The Unique Voice of
HILLARY RODHAM CLINTON:

A Portrait in Her Own Words

edited by
Claire G. Osborne

AVON BOOKS  NEW YORK

AVON BOOKS
A division of
The Hearst Corporation
1350 Avenue of the Americas
New York, New York 10019

Copyright © 1997 by Bill Adler
Interior design by Kellan Peck
Visit our website at **http://AvonBooks.com**
ISBN: 0-380-97461-9

Library of Congress Cataloging in Publication Data:
Clinton, Hillary Rodham.
    The unique voice of Hillary Rodham Clinton : a portrait in her own words / edited by Claire G. Osborne.
        p.   cm.
    1. Clinton, Hillary Rodham.   2. Presidents' spouses—United States—Biography.
3. Clinton, Hillary Rodham—Quotations.   I. Osborne, Claire G.   II. Title.
E887.C55083   1997
973.929'092—dc21
[B]   96-46399
                                                                          CIP

First Avon Books Printing: February 1997

AVON TRADEMARK REG. U.S. PAT. OFF. AND IN OTHER COUNTRIES, MARCA REGISTRADA, HECHO EN U.S.A.

Printed in the U.S.A.

OPM   10   9   8   7   6   5   4   3   2

*W*e are most grateful to Virginia Fay for her
creative efforts in assisting us in putting
this book together.

*W*e also would like to acknowledge the
research assistance of Patricia A. Ettrick.

This is a portrait of Hillary Rodham Clinton in her own words. Nothing portrays Hillary Rodham Clinton better than the words she has spoken and written about her life, her family, her career and her role as first lady.

Contents

Early Life

LOOKING BACK

Hillary Diane Rodham was born on October 26, 1947.

From a 1991 interview:

"I was born in Chicago and my parents moved to a suburb called Park Ridge when I was very young. Mostly because they wanted to be in a good school district. I mean, that's what the motivation was for the ex-GIs after World War II . . . to try to find a good place to raise your kids and send them to school.

"I had two younger brothers. We all went to public schools, had a superb public school education. I really felt well prepared."

"I was thinking one day how I used to get on my bicycle in the morning with my friends, and my mother would say, 'Well, be back in time for dinner.' And we'd go to each other's house; we'd go to the park; we would just ride around. And nobody was concerned about us. They had told us the obvious things about, you know, stay away from strangers and the like. But people expected their children to be safe at the end of the day. And that is practically impossible in most parts of our country now. So there are many ways in which the country has changed that I think we, as parents—and I'd say particularly as mothers—have to band together to get those conditions back. It is not fair to children that they are put into this kind of a situation. And, you know, I think there are many, many ways that we organize our lives that makes it especially difficult for parents to do the job they want with their children."

"As a girl, growing up in the forties and fifties, to have both a mother and a father who basically said, 'You can do or be whatever you choose, as long as you're willing to work for it,' was an unusual message."

"I guess that's one of the things that I look back on now with such great fondness, because there were always adults around who would care about you and would pick you up when you fell. I mean, they might not give you much sympathy, but they would be there for you. And they would tell you to keep going and not get deterred, and I just see so many kids today who don't have that kind of support."

"President Kennedy had just started the drive to the moon and this was, like, in 1961, and I was, like, fourteen or so. So I wrote a letter to NASA and asked them what you would do to be an astronaut. I told them something about myself."

(NASA wrote back that they were not accepting girls as astronauts. She found this "infuriating.")

"I later realized that I couldn't have been an astronaut anyway because I have such terrible eyesight. That somewhat placated me."

Her Parents

"My parents gave me my belief in working hard, doing well in school and not being limited by the fact that I was a little girl. It really was the classic parenting situation, where the mother is the encourager and helper, and the father brings news from the outside world. My father would come home and say, 'You did well, but could you do better? It's hard out there.' Encouragement was tempered with realism."

"I was a quick learner. I didn't run afoul of my parents very often. They were strict about my respecting authority, and not just parental authority. My father's favorite saying was: 'You get in trouble at school, you get in trouble at home.'"

She said her parents . . .

". . . told me it was my obligation to go to school, that I had an obligation to use my mind. They told me that an education would enable me to have a lot more opportunities in life, that if I went to school and took it seriously and studied hard, not only would I learn things and become interested in the world around me, but I would open up all kinds of doors to myself so that, when I was older, I would have some control over my environment."

Her Mother, Dorothy Howell Rodham

"I write about this in the book [*It Takes a Village*] and it was one of the things that I really had to think carefully about and ask her permission, because she is also a very private person. But I wanted to make the point that she had a very difficult childhood; a fifteen-year-old mother, a seventeen-year-old father. They were married, but that was a mere formality. They were immature, not ready for parenthood, very neglectful of her. When she was five she had a little sister. Her little sister was mistreated. And finally, her father, who then was about twenty-five, did make a good decision on her behalf, which was to get her out of the family environment. But he sent her and her little sister to California from Chicago on a train alone. And when I first heard that story I could not believe it, and to think about, you know, my child at eight taking care of a three-year-old little sister, being alone on a train. Unfortunately, the destination was not what one would

4

hope. Her grandparents were very severe, very rigid and arbitrary. Again, I think any fair reading would be 'mistreated'—both my mother and her sister. So when my mother was, I think, fourteen, she left her grandparents' home and went to work taking care of someone else's children. She was able to finish high school, but it was a very difficult childhood.

"So I think any one of us, if we look honestly at our own families, knows there no is picture-perfect family.

"All the way along, you could see that she wasn't getting what you would hope you'd get from a mother and a father. But she was having other adults there to help her. She had a teacher who would buy an extra carton of milk and leave it on the desk and say, 'Dorothy, I'm just full. I can't drink that today.' And the woman whose house she moved into, yes, she made her work, but she also taught her a lot.

"So if you're in your situation, we need to try to move you into a home where people will take care of you and where you can have a loving relationship. But we also need to be looking for ways we can help kids all the time. Every single adult can do something kind for a child and help that child on her way."

Remarks at the Mother of the Year Awards, May 1, 1995:

"My mother has always been there for me, and that is the greatest gift any child can receive from a parent. Of course, we don't always appreciate what it entails in being there with a child until we become mothers or fathers ourselves. I have discovered, certainly over the past fifteen years of my own daughter's life, that being a parent is a continuing learning process, a humbling experience, a continuing challenge and one that evolves and grows as your child does. I understand so much better a friend's description of mothers as 'every family's designated worrier.' "

"I would just add about my mother that she had a social conscience at a time when that was not even fashionable. She was always trying to make sure that we understood what was fair and what was just. She encouraged us to speak out and not worry about what anybody else thought, just to be ourselves."

Her Father, Hugh Rodham

"But always during my growing-up years and through college and beyond, what I loved and respected about my father is that he always took what I believed and cared about seriously, even when he disagreed very strongly. And there was always in our home an opportunity for the kind of discourse, one might say arguments, that mark people who care deeply and who have ideals."

"He said his prayers kneeling by his bed every night of his life, until he had [his] stroke."

On the death of her father in May 1993:

"When we got there, for the first couple of days, he knew we were there, and it was wonderful."

Asked how she's coping with her father's death:

"It comes up on you at odd times. I was in Montana—something I'd promised to do for a long time. I did not feel like going. I was so tired, drained, but I'm really glad I went, because the people were wonderful and a lot of them engaged me in talking about my father and were generally sympathetic. Today I feel pretty good. I feel we're back to settling in and trying to get rooted again."

Higher Education

WELLESLEY

"I went to Wellesley College, which is a women's college outside of Boston. I don't know why I chose that, other than during my senior year I had two young teachers—one had graduated from Wellesley and the other graduated from Smith. They'd been assigned to teach in my high school, and they were so bright and smart and terrific teachers and they lobbied me hard to apply to those schools, which I had never thought of before. And then when I was accepted they lobbied me hard to go and be able to work out all of the financial and other issues associated with it.

"So I went to Wellesley, and it was another educational experience for me. I always was interested in school. My parents impressed upon me that education was absolutely the key to personal growth, development, success."

". . . all very rich and fancy and very intimidating to my way of thinking."

"When I was a senior at Wellesley I decided I wanted to go to law school and I applied to several law schools. I ended up going to Yale. All during my growing-up years I had a combined message of personal opportunity but also public responsibility—that there were obligations that people who were as lucky as I was owed society."

Commencement address, Wellesley, May 31, 1969:

"We are, all of us, exploring a world that none of us understands and attempting to create within that uncertainty. But there are some things we feel, feelings that our prevailing acquisitive and competitive corporate life . . . is not the way of life for us. . . . We're searching for more immediate, ecstatic and penetrating modes of living. . . . That attempt at forging for many of us. . . has meant coming to terms with our humanness. Within the context of a society that we perceive—now we can talk about reality, and I would like to talk about reality sometime, authentic reality, inauthentic reality, and what we have to accept of what we see—but our perception of it is that it hovers often between the possibility of disaster and the potentiality for imaginatively responding to men's needs."

"I was here on campus when Martin Luther King was murdered. My friends and I put on black armbands and went into Boston to march in anger and pain—feeling as many of you did after the acquittals in the Rodney King case."

YALE LAW SCHOOL

"I got into Harvard and I got into Yale, and actually I went to a cocktail reception at the Harvard Law School with a young man who was, I think, a second-year Harvard law student. And he introduced me to one of the legendary Harvard law professors by saying, 'Professor So-and-so, this is Hillary Rodham. She's trying to decide between us and our nearest competitor.' And this man, with his three-piece suit and his bow tie, looked at me and said, 'First of all, we have no nearest competitor, and, secondly, we don't need any more women.' And that's how I decided to go to Yale."

Speaking at Yale Law School in 1992 about her days there:

"There was a great amount of ferment and confusion about what was and wasn't the proper role of law school education. We would have great arguments about whether we were selling out because we were getting a law degree,

10

whether in fact we should be doing something else, not often defined clearly but certainly passionately argued. That we should somehow be 'out there,' wherever 'there' was, trying to help solve the problems that took up so much of our time in argument and discussion.

"Those were difficult and turbulent times, trying to reconcile the reasoned, ordered world we were studying with what we saw around us."

MEETING BILL CLINTON

"I kind of, you know, looked. He was good-looking. And I thought—you know, I kind of filed that thought away. And after a while, I got to meet him, and we were in a class together."

"As I was cutting through the student lounge at the Yale Law School, this voice, said, 'And not only that, we grow the biggest watermelons in the world.' And I said, 'Who is that?' And my friend said, 'Oh, that's Bill Clinton. That's all he ever talks about. He's from Arkansas.'"

Introducing herself to Bill Clinton:

"Look, if you're going to keep staring at me, then I'm going to keep looking back. And I think we ought to know each other's names. I'm Hillary Rodham."

11

Running into each other while registering for classes at Yale:

"He joined me in this long line, and we talked for an hour. When we got to the front of the line, the registrar said, 'Bill, what are you doing here? You already registered.' "

What attracted her to Bill Clinton:

"He wasn't afraid of me."

About Bill Clinton (to friend Steve Cohen) when they first met:

"There's lots of layers to him. He's more complex than I thought. The more I see him, the more I discover new things about him."

"He cared deeply about where he came from, which was unusual. He was rooted and most of us were disconnected."

"After we finished law school, we carried on a long-distance romance between Massachusetts and Arkansas that made money for the telephone companies but wasn't very satisfying for us."

"I have always tried to listen to that voice deep inside of you—the voice that tells you right from wrong. It's so easy to find yourself editing feelings and beliefs based on what people may think. You only have one life to live. I knew my relationship with Bill was very important to me."

"You know, my friends loved Bill, but they thought I was going to the end of the earth."

To a colleague on the Watergate staff:
"You know, Bill Clinton is going to be president of the United States someday!"

Early Career

CHILDREN'S DEFENSE FUND

In 1970, Time *magazine ran an article on Marian Wright Edelman, a Yale Law School graduate and the first black woman to pass the bar in Mississippi, of the Children's Defense Fund. Hillary Rodham was impressed:*

"In one of those strange twists of fate that enters all our lives if we're open to hear and to see them, I knew right away that I had to go to work for her."

WATERGATE STAFF

In 1974, she worked on the legal staff preparing impeachment proceedings against Nixon:

"The most tedious work was transcribing [the tapes]. I was kind of locked in this soundproof room with these big headphones on, listening to a tape."

"I really didn't know what I wanted to do, but I wanted to get out of Washington. I was exhausted—we'd been working eighteen-, twenty-hour days. And when I had visited Bill, I had met the dean of the law school at Fayetteville and he had said to me, if you ever want to teach, let me know. So I figured, what the heck, it wouldn't hurt. So I picked up the phone. I called Wylie Davis, who was the dean at the law school. About August twentieth or so I pulled into Fayetteville, Arkansas, found out I was going to teach criminal law, was going to run a legal aid clinic, run a project that sent students down to the prisons to work with prison inmates. I was just kind of thrown into teaching right off the bat.

"Bill was, at that time, in the general election [for Congress]. So we had a very interesting first couple of months there, and I loved Fayetteville. I loved the university. I loved the law school. I loved my colleagues. I made some of the best friends I ever had in my life."

Arkansas

"I first came to Arkansas to visit Bill in 1973, to visit his family and see the state. And I was very taken by how beautiful it was. You know, he picked me up at the airport in Little Rock and we drove up Highway 7 and it was just beautiful. And then in 1973, when we both graduated from Yale, he came right home to Arkansas to teach in a law school and I was very unsure about where I wanted to be. I certainly was not ready to move completely to Arkansas yet, because I just didn't know whether that would be a decision that Bill would stick to. I really didn't know what to expect."

"It was never in the game plan to grow up and fall in love with someone from Arkansas. I had never known anyone from Arkansas."

"I had no choice but to follow my heart there [Arkansas]. Following your heart is never wrong."

"Once I got there, I made friends. I quickly became very comfortable. I liked people tapping me on the shoulder at the grocery store and saying, 'Aren't you that lady professor at the law school?'

"It was an adjustment in the sense that I'd never really lived in the South and I'd never lived in a small town, but I felt so immediately at home."

After a year of trying life in Arkansas, in the summer of 1975 she took a trip to visit friends in Park Ridge, Wellesley, Boston, New York and Washington.

"I went to Boston, New York, Washington, Chicago. I didn't see anything out there that I thought was more exciting or challenging than what I had in front of me."

"I think Arkansas is a wonderful place and filled with some of the best people I've ever been privileged to know or work with."

17

Marriage

Bill Clinton and Hillary Rodham were married on October 11, 1975:

"My relationships and my commitment to those relationships are the most important part of my life. I came to Arkansas because I loved Bill Clinton. He was a defeated politician when I married him."

"We spent a lot of time talking about our religious faith and beliefs.

"We, of course, think the most important thing is your personal relationship with God, and the denomination you belong to is a means of expressing that and being part of a fellowship."

Arkansas Politics, the Gubernatorial Years

In 1978, at age thirty-two, Bill Clinton became governor of Arkansas:

"Bill wanted to slay every dragon he could find. I mean, he took on every special interest group. He was ready to right every wrong that came his way. We were all young."

In 1979, Clinton named Hillary to head the Rural Health Advisory Committee, a forty-four-member board established to develop a program to deliver health care to people in isolated communities:

"If I were a man, they would probably say what a great, strong person this fellow is, how commanding he is, and all the rest. . . . I'm not reluctant to say what's on my mind, and if some people interpret that one way instead of another, I can't help that."

Interview with the Arkansas Gazette, *July 22, 1990:*

"Suppose I'd sat down and tried to map out my life. Do you suppose I would have said I'd be married to the governor of Arkansas and practicing law in Little Rock? No way."

"Bill Clinton has a record of accomplishment in a state that is a very small state. It's like living in a fishbowl, a very happy fishbowl, but nevertheless a small one, where people know him and they know him very, very well. And they've given him their trust and their confidence for eleven years in the highest position they could vote for him for."

About the five terms they were in Arkansas:

"We've had to deal with a lot of dirt and negative advertising. We've learned our lesson about how you stand up, answer your critics, and then just counterpunch as hard as you can. That's what we'll do in this campaign."

Hillary Who?

"I kept my maiden name when I married because it was important to me that I be judged on my merits and that Bill be judged on his merits . . . but I was not at all prepared about the concern people expressed about this decision, which we had made personally."

The name became a bigger problem:

"It became a kind of growing concern among supporters, who came to see me in droves, or called me on the phone and related story after story, and said, 'We really wish you would think about this.' "

On keeping her maiden name and then changing it (after Clinton lost the 1980 gubernatorial election—he was reelected in 1982):

"After the 1980 election a number of people said to me that it really bothered them and so I decided that I would, you know, add Clinton and go by Hillary Rodham Clinton. It was not a decision that was easy to make for me, but it was one that I made, thinking it was the best for me and the best for my husband."

She gave up using her maiden name after Clinton lost his bid for a second term as governor because voters resented the feminist image:

"I gave it up. It meant more to them than it did to me."

Bill Clinton never asked her to stop using her maiden name:

"I joked one time that probably the only man in Arkansas who didn't ask me to change my name was my husband— who said, 'This is your decision and you do exactly what you want.' And so I did. I just decided that it was not an issue that was that big to me when it came right down to it."

BABY CHELSEA

Chelsea Victoria Clinton was born on February 27, 1980:

"We were really anxious to have children. And so when I became pregnant, we were just thrilled. From the very beginning, Bill was so committed to being involved.

"We ended up having a Cesarean. And Bill was the first father they ever let into the operating room. They weren't going to let him in because they were afraid he'd get in their way or faint or something.

21

"Oh, yes, I was awake, and he was holding my hand. And then he started talking to all the doctors and nurses. And so it was just this kind of group experience. We were so happy from the very beginning. We would have loved to have more children."

Explaining the choice of their daughter's name (they had decided during the previous summer, just after Hillary had learned she was pregnant):

"It was this glorious morning [in England]. We were going to brunch and we were walking through Chelsea—you know, the flowerpots were out and everything. And Bill started singing 'It's a Chelsea Morning,' the Judy Collins song."

"I remember when I was breast-feeding Chelsea when I was still in the hospital. I had her head tilted at a funny angle and the milk started to come out of her nose. I thought I was killing my baby. I was just in a panic, you know, I was just really upset. And this wonderful old nurse came in and said, 'Well, if you hold her up a little higher, that won't happen.' "

"Bill was amazed by fatherhood. He was overwhelmed by it. I've heard him say that when he saw the child, he realized it was more than his own father could do."

"One of the things that Bill used to talk about a lot when Chelsea was born is how he never saw his own father, who was killed before he reached the age that Bill was when we had Chelsea. So to learn to be a father, he really had to be dedicated; he didn't have a model, and he certainly didn't have a model for fathering a daughter."

"I think that we both learned from Chelsea. I remember one night when she was just a few weeks old, and I was rocking her because she was crying. I just looked at her and said, 'Chelsea, you've never been a baby before, and I've never been a mother before, and we're just going to have to help each other get through this.' I think that our willingness to just learn from Chelsea and respect who she is, the person she was meant to be, has helped us a lot."

PARENTHOOD

"I have tried very hard to put my obligation to my daughter ahead of everything. And one of the things I have tried to do is make sure she not only had the support she needed but the time she needed."

"Seeing our daughter grow has been the great joy of our lives."

"I would have loved to have had more children, but it just didn't work out, so I have the best child there is."

Asked if they have considered adopting:

"We continue to talk about it. Because we really believe in adoption, and I have worked hard to promote adoption, particularly for older kids and across racial lines and kids with special needs. We'd have to think hard, especially if it were an older child, about the pressures of the White House on a child like that. We've thought about it."

About Chelsea as an only child:

"We'd always hoped to have another child, and so I was a little concerned about whether we would do enough for her to make life as rich as it needed to be. So we've always welcomed her friends, we've always encouraged her to spend a lot of time at our house or their houses to give her as broad a circle of people who cared about her as we possibly could and to encourage her to be involved."

24

ON BEING A WORKING MOTHER

"I was so exhilarated to have given birth to Chelsea that I vowed to do everything possible for her and to have her above anything else in my life. My mother had done that for me, and I never stopped being grateful for that. But that didn't mean I'd be a round-the-clock, stay-at-home mother."

She was fortunate that her office was five minutes from home:

"I could actually take a baby break instead of a lunch or coffee break and come home and feed Chelsea."

"When Chelsea was four or five, she went through a stage of asking 'Why do you have to go to work?' Ah, there's the guilt that strikes your heart. I don't know any mother who doesn't have pangs sometimes about leaving. There are times when a child badly wants more of you. I took Chelsea to the office when I could. She went to Bill's, too. There was a corner in his office that was hers, with crayons and paper where she could do coloring. I took work home a lot and did it after she was in bed."

25

Clinton Family Values

"As I look back at the level of confidence my parents instilled in me because of the way they raised me, I am trying the best I can to replicate that with my daughter. It's a wonderful gift to feel so loved and so special and supported, but also to be given the kind of discipline and direction to find your way in life."

"The only thing [Bill and I] can do is to try to develop our own values and our own sense of who we are. That's what Bill and I were raised to believe about ourselves, and that's what we're going to try to do for our daughter. And I think that's the best gift you can give a child, some internal compass. It's not pleasant when people say or do things that are cruel, but that's more a reflection on them than on my daughter or me or my husband. And that's what we're trying to help her understand."

"The trips we've been able to take as a family and then the trips that she and I have taken on behalf of the president have been some of the best times in my life."

"I need to spend quiet time with Chelsea. What I care about most in this world is my family."

"One of the reasons I came home so much [during the 1992 campaign] was not only to see how she was but to recharge my batteries, which she was a big part of doing. We just spent a lot of time together, and really it was important for me. I took her to school, I took her shopping, we watched videos, we both just kind of refueled our own energy level so that we could both keep going in it."

"I know that my daughter's life has been influenced and affected by countless other people, some of whom I know; many, many others I will never meet. Think of it: the police who patrol our streets to keep our children safe; the government officials who monitor the quality of air and water and food; the business leaders who employ parents and make decisions about what kind of income and benefits they will receive; the executives who produce the programs that our children see on television.

"As adults we have to start thinking and believing that there isn't really any such thing as someone else's child. My child, your child, all children everywhere must live and make their ways in society. And now, in the increasingly shrinking world we live in, in the larger globe as well."

"One night we just got into this silly conversation, just the three of us. Chelsea had to memorize all of the members of the cabinet, and it was just hysterical. We were rhyming them and making acronyms, and it was so much fun. So we've had some good times as well as some hard times."

Her Mother-in-law,
Virginia Dell Cassidy Blythe Clinton Dwire Kelley

"The first time I met her was when Bill and I were students at Yale Law School and she came to New Haven, Connecticut, for a visit. I had never seen somebody in real life who wore false eyelashes every day."

"We were utterly different. Like the characters in *Star Trek*, Virginia Kelley and I seemed to be from different planets."

After the death of Virginia's third husband, Jeff Dwire:

"Dear Virginia:

Here are copies of the eulogy Bill delivered for Jeff and the original Bill wrote and spoke from. He made a few minor changes that show up in the typed version. I think every day about you and Jeff. With Bill, I can honestly say I never knew a better man than Jeff. I also have never known a more generous and stronger woman than you. You're an inspiration to me and so many others. In addition, you're just as good a politician as your son. After he wins, we'll have to decide what position you'll seek. If there's anything I can do for you, please let me know.

Be well.

> Love,
> Hillary"

"The other thing I would say about Bill's mother, which was really remarkable, is that she was able to love lots of people unconditionally. Sometimes I would say to her, 'How can you stand that person?' And she'd say, 'Oh, he's good to his mother' or 'She's good to her dog.' She had a capacity to find something good about people. And that love enabled her to reach so many people and to give them the gift of her spirit."

"Unlike many people, Virginia didn't try to control her fate. And in the end she was really able to live life—and finish life—on her own terms."

Virginia Clinton Kelley died on January 6, 1994:

"Virginia's greatest legacy was to show that, even in the midst of personal trials and pain, you can and must keep going. Her lesson was that no matter how hard life gets, you get up in the morning, say a prayer, put a smile on your face, and go out and brave the world to do the best that you can—with or without false eyelashes.''

HILLARY RODHAM CLINTON, ATTORNEY AT LAW

''I thought maybe I'd practice law when I got to Little Rock, but there were not any women lawyers, period.''

On being the family breadwinner:

''It was something we knew was inevitable if we were going to be in public life in Arkansas, because salaries were the lowest in the country. It does weigh heavily. I think from time to time it was a pretty substantial burden on me personally. But in the balance of our marriage, it was something I was glad to do. . . . And because I tried very hard not to be compensated at all through my law firm for any representation my firm did that could in any way be related to the state, I voluntarily suppressed my income for years and years.''

Regarding conflict of interest charges (that she helped a savings and loan represented by her law firm get a break from the state board appointed by her husband):

''This is the sort of thing that happens to women who have their own careers.''

"For goodness sake, you can't be a lawyer if you don't represent banks."

"You know, I was a lawyer for twenty years. I think like a lawyer. That is not often the best thing for somebody in my position. I recognize that."

EDUCATION REFORM

In 1983, Bill Clinton decided to reform Arkansas's education system and put Hillary in charge. She was named by her husband to the Arkansas Education Standards Committee:

"One of the principal problems we face in our state, and apparently in the country, is that we are not expecting enough of ourselves, our schools, or our students.

"We have an obligation to challenge our students and to set high expectations for them. Rather than setting minimum standards, we should set expectations and urge schools and districts to aim to achieve those expectations and not to be satisfied with meeting some artificial minimum."

On teacher competency testing:

"I think we have to hit head-on the widespread public belief that we have a lot of incompetent teachers because

I don't think we can build a constituency for education unless we do confront that . . . I think it will clear the air of a lot of misconceptions and inaccuracies about our teachers."

The Education Standards Committee completed its work on December 10, 1983, and it was presented on March 1:

"I think we have a really good set of standards, a blueprint that Arkansas can follow over the next few years. This is a move toward competency-based education and the requirement of more accountability and responsibility from students, teachers, the school systems and parents."

The Educational Standards Committee released its preliminary report on September 6, 1983. Hillary spoke at a press conference:

"Our schools are not doing as good a job as they must. While there may be many causes for our dilemma, there is only one solution. We Arkansans have to quit making excuses and accept instead the challenge of excellence once and for all.

"[A school that] passes illiterate or semiliterate students commits educational fraud. There is a feeling of urgency and a need for changes in education. If we do not seize the opportunity we have now, we will go backward."

"The road to being somebody in this society starts with education, and we intend to be sure that everybody in this room and every child in this state is somebody. Because we're going to give them every chance we can to develop their minds so that they can play a role in this state and this country to make it the kind of place it needs to be."

In 1985, she helped start HIPPY, the Home Instruction Program for Preschool Youngsters, a program in which aides and tutors go into homes to teach impoverished mothers how to teach their four- and five-year-olds at home:

"It became clear to me that we could have the most astonishing schools in the world and we would still not be reaching the needs of all of our children, because half of all learning occurs by the time a person is five. And the way that our children are treated in the first five years—the way their health is attended to, to say nothing of intellectual stimulation and family support—will have a very big influence on how well they can do for the rest of their lives."

NOTE: HIPPY originated at Hebrew University in Jerusalem during the 1960s and was designed to prepare preschool children of immigrants in basic skills required to tackle education programs in public schools. The premise was to have mothers prepare their children at home.

"I am just absolutely convinced that an investment in pre-school is one of the smartest investments Arkansas can make. The single biggest determinant, based on the studies that I've seen, as to whether a child finished school and how well that child does, is the educational level of the mother. And a mother doesn't have to be, herself, well educated to see that her child succeeds, but she has to understand the value of education."

Presidential Politicking

CAMPAIGNING

1988

> *Clinton considered a run for the presidency in 1988. She pointed out that he was . . .*

" . . . very deliberative when faced with a difficult decision. I have no doubts that he would be an excellent president."

> *Clinton decided against a 1988 run for the presidency, saying it was because of Chelsea's young age (she was seven at the time):*

"Well, what you do when you're trying to make the decision, you have to proceed as if you're doing it. You have to decide, can I raise the money? Can I put together the organization? Do I have a message that the people would be receptive to? And in the process of going about those things, you are sending off the signals that you are running, but then, even after you go through all that, there comes a point where you say, 'Okay, do I want to do that now?' And when they sat down, they decided the answer was, 'No, not now.' Looking back on it, he was right. That wasn't the time."

1992

On the possibility of a run for president in 1992:

"I haven't thought about it very seriously because I don't think it's a very likely possibility. Bill is personally very capable, obviously, along with a number of qualified Democrats who would be certainly in a position to do an excellent job. But what's more important to me is that we have something to say and that we have policies that are responsive to the needs of people."

"We're thinking about doing it. We're thinking about going forward with this great adventure. What do you all think?

"Bill made a contract with the people of Arkansas to not run and he's really worried about it."

"We believe passionately in this country and we cannot stand by for one more year and watch what is happening to it."

"If you vote for my husband, you get me; it's a two-for-one, blue-plate special."

"I have never thought that it was going to be an easy campaign, or that the kinds of issues and changes that Bill Clinton was advocating would be easily understood or accepted by everybody. And you know—remember, Abraham Lincoln was the first person who said that you can't please all of the people all of the time. But what we're interested in is trying to convince a majority of Americans to understand what's at stake in this election. And I feel such a personal obligation to help my husband on this and to try to stand up and say what we think is going on in the country, and then to try to bring about changes that will help people. So I'm sure there are people who are not going to approve or understand, and I just hope that most people will listen and think, 'Why are these two doing this,' you know? 'Why is Bill Clinton putting himself on the line like this?' And it's because he's really committed to making the changes this country needs."

Campaigning:

"There's not much inherent attractiveness in turning your life over to this process."

Consultant Paul Begala's wife was eight months pregnant; Hillary and Bill Clinton insisted he go home for a month with full pay:

"This is the most important thing that will ever happen to you, not the election."

"You know, every time Bill Clinton gets ahead, the people that are running against him attack him, and I think that that's because the issues in this campaign really will cause change in this country."

During the 1992 campaign, she frequently returned home to Little Rock to . . .

". . . make a cup of tea, hang out with Chelsea, take an afternoon nap. If I don't get back there, I don't feel grounded."

Asked if she thought the campaign would get nasty:

"Oh, I hope not. You know, I really wish everybody in the Republican operation would reread Lee Atwater's article in *Life* magazine before he died, when he regretted the kind of negative campaigning he'd been part of running, both the Reagan and Bush campaigns, and really called on all of us to love—maybe love each other a little more, care about each other, and get away from that kind of politics. But if they don't read it or they don't heed it and they come after us, then we'll answer, because we know that that's required, but then we'll try to get back on subject, which is America's future—not Bill or Al or Tipper or me, because we consider ourselves kind of instruments for change in this time when it's so desperately needed."

During the campaign of 1992, they gave the press the slip during a visit to New York City:

"We went to Times Square to see *My Cousin Vinny,* and we fooled everyone. We bought lots of popcorn, hot dogs, nachos—and diet Cokes to salve our consciences."

"We've had to create time. We were doing well for years, until this campaign. We'd go to the movies together, have dates together . . . Bill and I are such moviegoers; we've gone to five o'clock, seven o'clock and nine o'clock shows all in one night."

Asked what has surprised her most about the campaign:

"Gee, I think the biggest surprise is what a disconnection there is between what people ask me and how the campaign is covered."

About rumors of infidelity by President Bush:

"Nobody knows better than I how painful discussions of rumors can be. I wouldn't want anybody else, and I certainly don't want the Bush family, subjected to that."

About discussing the rumors about Bush:

"It was a mistake. Nobody knows better than I the pain that can be caused by even discussing rumors in private conversation. And I did not mean to be hurtful to anyone.

"I shouldn't have been drawn into a discussion under any circumstances. It was in a private conversation, but that's not the point. After what my husband and I have been through, I don't think the media should go after anybody."

On her possible future role in her husband's administration:

"Bill might appoint a commission, maybe on children and strengthening families. I don't know exactly what form my commitment would take, but that's an idea that would make sense."

"If Bill is elected, it will be hard, if not impossible, for me to continue to practice law. There are legitimate questions of conflict of interest."

"I am pursuing the goals I always envisioned, perhaps with more success here."

She expects to . . .
" . . . be involved in helping to bring about changes in those areas in which I have an abiding interest. How? I don't know yet. . . . It may not be that I would be practicing law in a private firm. But I would be using my legal expertise to help resolve problems."

"I don't want to be paid. It's not possible. I've learned how sensitive people are to potential conflict and breaches of trust."

"You know, I want to do what is right for me in terms of the contribution that I can make. And I really believe right now we need a comprehensive children and family agenda in this country. And the way I think about it is what do I try to give my daughter? What I want to do is be a voice

41

for children in the White House. And by that I mean I want to marshal the resources. I want to help create the constituencies and implement the kind of agenda that would really make it possible for us to say we are not neglecting our children as a nation, which right now we cannot, with a straight face, say."

"The idea that I would check my brain at the White House door is something that just doesn't make any sense to me."

AL AND TIPPER GORE

"Well, she [Tipper] is the best friend. You know, when I think about how wonderful a relationship Bill and I have with Al and Tipper, and what a source of strength and support we've tried to be, all four of us, for each other, I don't know how presidents and vice presidents can carry the burden of the office without that kind of friendship and love that we feel toward each other. It's been one of the greatest gifts I've ever been given."

Bryant Gumbel: "You two have surely seen the widespread speculation that one campaign isn't big enough for two women as strong-willed and independent minded and outspoken as each of you are. You're laughing. How's that speculation strike you?"

"Well, Bryant, that always is sort of funny to me. I mean,

you know, I think both Tipper and I believe that this country's big enough for millions of women who are outspoken and concerned about what's going on, and we want every woman in this country to play a role in helping to change things for the better for herself and her family and, really, for all of us. So we view this as a terrific opportunity, because I feel that I've got support to do the kinds of things I think are important for children. I'm very interested in her issues, matters like mental health and the kinds of things we need to do to help our people get back on their feet again after a pretty dry spell for the last twelve years."

"They leave Al and Tipper alone. I mean, Al and Tipper go to all their kids' games. And I think Bill deserves to have some of that same space and have some normal family life."

IT'S THE ECONOMY, STUPID

"Now, remember back six years, ten years, to what we in this part of the country thought of as economic development. We thought it consisted of enticing someone from somewhere else to come here. 'Smokestack chasing' is what it was often called. If we could just convince someone to get out of 'crummy old dying Detroit' or Chicago and move to Kentucky or Tennessee or Arkansas or Georgia, we were going to be moving right along. Of course, in the last six years, we have seen how many of those industries that we got to move from Chicago and Detroit have moved on to Taiwan and Bangladesh. And we have seen something more important—that economic development cannot depend on what kind of jobs we bring here as much as on what we do to invest in our people, to become more self-sufficient, to generate more of our own economic opportunities."

"We've got to have a long-term strategy to change this economy and start investing in people again. We have to get a hold of our banking system. Bill has said if he were president, among the things he would do would be to fully fund Head Start."

Commencement address to the University of Michigan, May 1, 1993:

"We really are at a fork in the road. Will we end the denial of the last years in which everything was fine and those on the top prospered, while those in the middle and the poor saw their opportunities diminish? Will we continue to live in a sense of unreality that we don't have to get our deficit down, we don't have to balance our budget, we don't have to provide jobs for people who, through no fault of their own, are being replaced by machines and automation and robots? Will we take on the challenges of our disintegrating family structure and our violent communities? I think we will. And I think the class of 1993 will be there to make sure that we do."

Speech at the Greater Detroit Chamber of Commerce, June 1, 1995:

"If one asks, as I have for a number of years, business leaders across our country, I don't think the answers I heard elsewhere are any different from what you would tell me about what you need to compete in the new global economy. You need an educated, healthy, productive workforce."

"Governments are responsible for promoting disciplined economic politics. They must strengthen the conditions that sustain democracy and market economies that we know can unleash the creative energies of millions of people—if these people are prepared to take advantage of the opportunities available to them."

Speech at the Greater Detroit Chamber of Commerce, June 1, 1995:

"What we should be about the business of trying to do in all of our individual capacities is both to make sure people have the opportunity to make a decent wage, to have incomes that will support themselves, and at the same time to try and reinforce values that support and strengthen families. That is what we have tried to do in the last couple of years. It is a very big task. It is not a task that can be accomplished by any particular sector of our society acting alone. It is not a partisan task. It is an American challenge.''

Campaign Crises

Tea and Cookies

"I suppose I could have stayed home and baked cookies and had teas, but what I decided to do is fulfill my profession. The work that I have done as a professional, a public advocate, has been aimed . . . to assure that women can make the choices . . . whether it's a full-time career, full-time motherhood, or some combination.''

"Now, the fact is, I've made my share of cookies and served hundreds of cups of tea. But I never thought that made me a good, bad, or indifferent mother, or a good or bad person. So it never occurred to me that my comment would be taken as insulting mothers (I guess including my own!) who choose to stay home with their children full-time. Nor did it occur to me that the next day's headlines would reduce me to an anti-family 'career woman.' ''

"I have yet to meet a woman who doesn't have some ambivalence. Introduce her to me, if you will, because I think most women, as they go through their lives, face a lot of tough choices. And I was saying nothing at all about women who choose to stay home and are full-time mothers and homemakers. And I regret that anybody thought I was. Because anyone who knows me, and knows the kind of work I've done now for many years, knows that part of what I'm trying to accomplish is to provide more opportunities for more women to choose that full-time homemaking and mothering role, if that's what the choice is. I think it's important for women to respect each others' choices. There are enough stresses in today's life without setting up camps against one another and pointing fingers at each other. And I hope that any woman who's listening this morning, who took the comment out of context or didn't know what I was responding to, will know that that is not at all what I meant.''

"Stand by Your Man"

''You know, I'm not sitting here like some little woman standing by her man like Tammy Wynette. I'm sitting here because I love him and I respect him and I honor what he's been through and what we've been through together. And, you know, if that's not enough for people, then, heck, don't vote for him.''

''I didn't mean to hurt Tammy Wynette as a person. I happen to be a country-western fan. If she feels like I've hurt her feelings, I'm sorry about that.''

The Clinton Marriage

"Bill and I have always loved each other. No marriage is perfect, but just because it isn't perfect doesn't mean the only solution is to walk off and leave it. A marriage is always growing and changing. We couldn't just say, 'Well, this isn't ideal,' and get a divorce. I'm proud of my marriage. I have women friends who chose not to marry, or who married and chose not to have children, or who married and then divorced, or who had children on their own. That's okay, that's their choice. This is my choice. This is how I define my personhood—it's Bill and Chelsea."

"If you're married for more than ten minutes, you're going to have to forgive somebody for something. And that's one of the things we've had to learn over sixteen years. There are a lot of big and little things that come up in a marriage that if you don't deal with right then and there, they can sink you."

Asked if she thought her husband had told her everything she needed to know:

"Yes, I have absolutely no doubt about that. I don't think I could be sitting here otherwise. That's been, over years, part of the development of trust."

"We were never going to go apart. We just had to deal with the issues in our marriage and work them out. We just talked to each other and a few close friends."

"I feel very lucky because Bill and I have matured together. We've been through a lot. We've always loved and respected each other, yet even with that it has not been easy. Every marriage requires 100 percent effort by each spouse. It's not fifty-fifty, and that's a hard lesson to learn. But it's worth the sacrifice and work."

"From my perspective, our marriage is a strong marriage. We love each other."

During the famous 60 Minutes *interview, January 26, 1992:*

"I don't want to be any more specific. I don't think being any more specific about what's happened in the privacy of our life together is relevant to anybody besides us."

Katie Couric: "How much influence do you have?"

"I don't know that I have any more influence than anybody else who is an adviser to the president, and there are dozens of people whom he talks to on a regular basis and asks advice from, just as he always has. . . .

"But I think that everybody who's in any kind of marriage, and particularly the marriages that have lived inside this house, knows that husbands and wives influence each other. That's just our common everyday experience."

There were some stories in the press that she had thrown a lamp or a Bible at her husband:

"A lamp or a Bible or a Mercedes Benz, or, you know, there were many variations on it. When stories like that get into what I consider to be respectable journalism, it does bother me, and it particularly bothered me that the Secret Service was being used to try to substantiate untrue stories and I couldn't understand that. So I was concerned about it and expressed that concern."

Barbara Walters: "Did you ask to have certain Secret Service members put in another detail?"

"No. No. I wanted the situation cleared up because—both for the Secret Service's sake, which is, after all, charged with a very difficult task and we have a great relationship with them, but also for my sake. I mean, you know, I have a pretty good arm. If I'd thrown a lamp at somebody, I think you would have known about it, and, you know, when those things are said, I just don't want that to get a life of its own."

RUMORED INFIDELITIES

Charges of her husband's infidelities brought this comment:

"I find it not an accident that every time he is on the verge of fulfilling his commitment to the American people and they are responding . . . out comes yet a new round of these outrageous, terrible stories that people plant for political and financial reasons."

Asked if fidelity has been a problem in their marriage:

"I don't talk about it. I think my marriage is my marriage and my relationship with my husband is solely between us."

On charges of Bill Clinton's womanizing, and the press:

"It hurts. Even though you're a public figure, which means apparently in America anybody can say anything about you. Even public figures have feelings and families and reputations."

51

Gennifer Flowerd, et al.

"It's not true. I just don't believe any of that. All of these people, including that woman, have denied this many, many times. I'm not going to speculate on her motive. We know she was paid."

Interview with Sam Donaldson:

"Well, I'll tell you what. This was a woman who at least pretended that her life was ruined because somebody had alleged that she had a relationship at some point with Bill Clinton.

"Anybody who knows my husband knows that he bends over backwards to help people who are in trouble and is always willing to listen to their problems.

"The first time he called her, I mean, we were in the kitchen together and he said, you know, 'This woman thinks her life is over,' and he felt very sorry for her."

ABC News Primetime Live, *January 30, 1992:*

"If somebody's willing to pay you $130,000 or $170,000 to say something and you get your fifteen minutes of fame and you get your picture on the front page of every newspaper and you're some failed cabaret singer who doesn't even have much of a résumé to fall back on, and what's there, she's lied about—you know, that's the daughter of

Willie Horton, as far as I'm concerned. It's the same kind of attempt to keep the real issues of this country out of the mainstream debate where they need to be."

"We now know that when Republicans first offered money to this woman [Gennifer Flowers] to change her story she held out, apparently negotiating with the media, *Star* magazine, to change a story she had denied repeatedly."

"If we'd been in front of a jury I'd say, 'Miss Flowers, isn't it true you were asked this by AP in June of 1990 and you said no? Weren't you asked by the *Arkansas Democrat* and you said no?' I mean, I would crucify her."

DIVORCE

"As I say in my book, I think getting a divorce should be much harder when children are involved."

Interview with David Frost during the 1992 campaign, talking about the troubles in their marriage and asked if they had considered divorce:

"Not seriously . . . no, no . . . I mean . . . I never doubted and I know he never did either, that not only do we love each other but that we are committed to each other. That love was something so much a part of us that it was impossible to think of ending or cutting it off or moving beyond it."

"My strong feelings about divorce and its effects on children have caused me to bite my tongue more than a few times during my own marriage and to think instead about what I could do to be a better wife and partner. My husband has done the same."

1994 ELECTIONS

Accepting an award from the National Women's Law Center after the 1994 election, in which Republicans won:

"In many ways, our best days are ahead of us because there's nothing like a good fight for advocates to get energized."

On the Contract with America:

"Oh, I think it's a very good organizing tool, and I complement those people who came up with the idea. But like many contracts, you have to read the fine print, and sometimes when it's implemented, it's not exactly what it was apparently going to be, and I think that's where we are right now in the country."

1996

On her husband's chances for reelection:

"Because he's right about what's going on in the country and in the world, and he takes risks—takes risks for peace, whether it's in Northern Ireland or Haiti. And he also tries to bring people together, not to divide them, and that's what this world needs right now. And in our hearts, when the real time comes to make decisions, people are going to vote for a peacemaker and a man of vision over politics as usual, and he will be reelected."

"I think what he does is bring to the campaign, as he brings to his presidency, strong feelings and values about what he wants to do in America, what he wants to stand up for. That's another part of the bum rap. I mean, here is somebody who has stood up to the National Rifle Association, to get the assault weapons ban and the Brady Bill, has stood up to the tobacco manufacturers on behalf of his campaign against teenage smoking. Has stood up time and again, against the majority in Congress, on behalf of whether it's Medicare, or Medicaid, or education or the environment. He has a very strong sense of where he thinks our country should go and that's where he has been leading us."

Asked on Newshour with Jim Lehrer, *May 28, 1996, if the "two-for-one" deal is still in effect:*

"I don't know. Do you think there's a fire sale somewhere? We could put it up on the wall. I don't have any idea. I mean, I find all of this a little bit, you know, funny, I suppose. My husband and I have been husband and wife and best friends and partners for a very long time. We work together. We support each other, and I think most married couples that stay together as long as we have are in the same boat. I mean, so, you know, I'm going to be there for him. I'm going to do whatever I can, and that's part of what I believe in, and that's what I'll be doing in this campaign."

At an Emily's List* luncheon:

"I just want, briefly, to run through the challenges that I see and I talk about and I listen to as others talk to me about. The first challenge is we have to cherish our children and strengthen our families. And that is work—that is work that women have always done, haven't we? Whether or not we have children of our own, we have helped to take care of both the young and the old. We look around, and we see the needs and we try to fulfill them. And so it is work that has to be done primarily on the individual level, but it makes a big difference who's in the White House and who's in the Congress."

About the 1996 presidential campaign:

"I will be very involved and active. All of us who care about the quality of life for ourselves and our children will be involved in it."

*Emily's List is an organization that raises money for female Democratic candidates who support abortion rights.

"I think that unfortunately a lot of our campaigns have gotten nasty and mean-spirited in the past years. Well, I think it's because when people do not have their own vision for what this country should do, don't have a positive program to help people get and keep jobs or provide health care, or better education, or keep the environment clean, then you're more likely to see a campaign based on personality. And I don't think that that's good news, but I hope that the American people will see it for what it is. And I have a lot of confidence in the American public and expect that will be what they'll do."

"I love campaigning. I love meeting people. I love listening to people. I always learn a lot. I feel like I'm in, you know, some kind of wonderful graduate education course."

Barbara Walters (on ABC News 20/20, January 12, 1996): "Do you think that you're becoming more of the negative than a positive force for your husband? Are you becoming a political liability?"

"Oh, I hope not because I love my husband and I really believe in what he's doing and I want to help him. But I have campaigned with him for, you know, gosh, ever since I've known him, and I'm going to do the same thing in this upcoming election. At the end of the day, the American people will know we have nothing to cover up, there is nothing that we have done that should be of any concern to anyone. We've tried, maybe not as smartly as we could have, to answer peoples' questions, but we'll keep doing the best we know how."

Politics

She was raised by Republicans, later worked for Eugene McCarthy in the 1968 New Hampshire primary, then Nelson Rockefeller at the Republican convention. She didn't consider herself a "liberal" who favored big government:

"Even at that early stage, I was against all these people who came up with these big government programs that were more supportive of bureaucracies than they were actually helpful to people. I've been on this kick for twenty-five years."

"If we've proved nothing else, we've proved we are resilient. We know how to fight; we can take these people on."

Speech in Los Angeles, March 26, 1995:

"We need to be against brain-dead politics wherever we

find it! We need to forge a new consensus about [our] new political direction . . . that doesn't jerk us to the right, jerk us to the left, prey on our emotions, engender paranoia and insecurity . . . but instead moves us forward together."

"Unless we all figure out how we're going to sustain a democracy in the information-overload age, I'm concerned about who will enter public life, who will stay in public life, the quality of decisions that are made, the extraordinary role that big moneyed interests will play because they can marshal information-driven campaigns that permeate the atmosphere with misinformation or, if not wrong information, [information that is] inaccurate because [it is] incomplete."

Responding to political attacks on her:

"I really don't know what to make of it. What recently has happened has been part of a very sad and cynical political strategy. It's not really about me. I find it hard to take a lot of that personally, since the portrait is a distorted, inaccurate one."

Commencement address at Drew University, Madison, N.J., May 18, 1996:

"I don't mean to suggest that government is perfect by any means. The practice of politics and governing has never been easy. Max Weber once said that politics is 'a strong and slow boring of hard boards.' I would add that sometimes it's just plain boring, and there doesn't seem to be any way around that because politics is not just about who's elected to office. Politics is how we get along with one another. How we compromise with each other. When someone says to me, 'How can you stand being involved in politics?' I always say, 'Are you married? Do you have a family? Do you belong to a church or school?' Because politics with a small *p* is that process that brings us together peaceably to work toward common ends."

"We demand much too much of our political people in terms of the way we expect them to live, the kinds of external, reactive lifestyles we expect them to have. We have really collapsed the space in which public people can live, to the detriment of our overall politics. That's the way it is in this country. You lose not just privacy—you lose the opportunity to be a real person."

"I never believe polls—good, bad, indifferent."

REPUBLICANS

"I feel like my political beliefs are rooted in the conservatism that I was raised with. I don't recognize this new brand of Republicanism that is afoot now, which I consider to be very reactionary, not conservative in many respects.

61

I am very proud that I was a Goldwater girl. And then my beliefs changed over time. But I always thought that role of citizen, the role of advocate, was as important in our democracy as running for office."

"I love watching the Republicans squirm when the tables are turned. They are great at dishing it out, but they really can't take it when the truth is pointed out about them."

"We have such a schizophrenic view toward politics—people claim they want somebody to tell them the truth, to be tough, make hard decisions. But they don't want it to be painful. Reagan had such a hold on the popular imagination, he could have asked something from people, but he squandered an extraordinary political opportunity.

"At least he had some core beliefs. They defied logic, but at least he had them. He was followed by someone who didn't."

"I met President Nixon only once, when he came to the White House to speak with the president about Russia prior to the meeting with Yeltsin. He came to the second floor, where my daughter and I were waiting to greet him, and he had prepared what he was going to say to both of us, so when he met Chelsea, he immediately began talking about her school, which both of his daughters had attended, and his memories of it. When he met me, he immediately talked about health care, and said, 'You are attempting to do now what I tried to do.' President Nixon had proposed a national health care plan. I was very impressed by his discipline in the way he had prepared just to say hello to us."

ON RUNNING FOR OFFICE HERSELF

"Since I was in eighth grade, people have been urging me to run for public office. People think that because I care so much about public issues, I should run for office myself. I don't want to run for office. In 1990, when it looked as though Bill might not run for governor, I had dozens of people call me and tell me to run. But it just wasn't anything I was interested in. An elected official has to deal with many things—I see the way Bill does it. Seven or eight different things in one day. And he's good at that. What I see for myself is a role as an advocate."

Asked if she would run for president:

"People have always talked to me about running, since high school. I have too many other things I'm interested in—my life, my daughter. But I like to be part of solving problems, like to see things happen. We shouldn't leave the work of politics to people who run for public office."

During the 1992 campaign:
"We'll have a woman president by 2010."

Asked if she'd consider running:
"We'll talk later."

PHILOSOPHY, POLITICAL AND OTHERWISE

Don Jones, her youth group mentor, wrote to her at Wellesley and questioned whether someone can be a Burkean realist about history and human nature and also have liberal sentiments and visions:

"It is an interesting question you posed—can one be a mind conservative and a heart liberal?"

To the Association of American Medical Colleges:
"It's about time we start thinking about the common good and the national interest, instead of just individuals in our country."

"We came of age in the civil rights movement, the Vietnam War, the women's movement, Watergate, an impeachment of a president. I mean, we've had—lived through, in our growing-up years, as many psychic shocks to the body politic as you can imagine. And a lot of us have had to really kind of find our way, make sense of the world that we're in. So I think from my perspective, where we are now, most of us in or approaching middle age—which is hard to say— most of us have come through pretty well."

"Because of crime, because of declining productivity, because of a declining tax base—you can list all of it. Personal security is at the root of everything that I think we have to be focused on. Personal security on the streets and in your homes, personal security to not worry about being sick and facing catastrophe, personal security in some job that we can hold out to the people.

"You can go down the line and nearly every issue we look at, whether it's instilling responsibility and self-esteem in children who are living in our inner cities or personal security to our elderly citizens who lock themselves behind their doors because of those same children. We are all in this together."

"Somebody said to me today that when you are in your middle years, you have more parents alive than children. I mean, that's just kind of phenomenal. I don't know if it's true, but it sure did strike me, because most of us are in this sandwich generation who'll deal with all these issues."

Remarks to the American Medical Association, June 13, 1993:

"Just as our institutions across society are under attack and stress, all elements of those institutions are finding that they no longer can command the trust and respect, whether we talk of parents or government officials or other professionals—police officers, teachers—that should come with giving of themselves and doing a job well that needs to be done."

"You know, you have a choice, whatever your circumstances are. You either become overwhelmed by life or you continue to try to challenge yourself to grow and enjoy the days that you're given—and that has always been the way I've lived. I'm not saying it's easy. I'm not saying there are not days when you wish for it all to go away and you can have some peace and quiet for maybe a week. But this is my life, and I'm very proud of my life."

Remarks at the ninth Annual Women in Policing Awards, August 10, 1994:

"We need to start rewarding people for making the tough decisions instead of just talking about them. We need to hold people accountable, so that if their rhetoric outpaces results, they know we're watching. We need to solve problems, not just talk about them. We need to reward people who go the extra mile, who stick their necks out, who take the risks."

Speech to the League of Women Voters, June 14, 1994:

"We are a diverse, wonderful collection of points of view and attitudes and backgrounds and experience. But we need to understand we are also very much connected by our shared humanity, and that it is time once again in America to care for each other, to reach out and help one another."

Speech at George Washington University, November 30, 1994:

"I know that in these days it's . . . not fashionable or politically correct, which now has a new meaning in Washington, to talk about mercy and to talk about kindness for the less fortunate, and particularly toward children, but I don't think a nation can be great that turns its back on the poor and the unfortunate and the children among us. And so, for me, that's what I would like to work for."

Speech at the Greater Detroit Chamber of Commerce, June 1, 1995:

"The best social program is a job. The best social policy is a robust economy. But one does not live by jobs and the economy alone. There is also a spiritual dimension to life. There is a sense of connection to life.''

Remarks at Brooklyn College Commencement, June 1, 1995:

''Education matters. Kindness matters. Truth matters. Patience, hard work, tolerance, discipline—all of these matter. Forgiveness matters and gratitude matters, especially on a day like today.''

Practicing ''the discipline of gratitude'':

''There was a book by Henri Nouwen, the Jesuit theologian, and it was about the prodigal son. And, you know, sometimes it's good to be reminded that people don't get what they think they deserve, that life is unfair, that every one of us is going to encounter obstacles. So, the whole book was helpful, but in it was this phrase, 'the discipline of gratitude,' and I had never thought of gratitude being a discipline. And I began to do that. I mean, every day, no matter what is happening around me, I consciously try to discipline my own feelings and my mind about what I have to be grateful for, because by any stretch of the imagination—even during the worst times, when people are accusing me of things and doing all that they do—I'm a very lucky person.''

"I mean, you look at those flowers and you think, 'My gosh, if my life were to end tomorrow, how lucky I've been that nearly all my life I've been surrounded by flowers.' "

"If you're not willing to make tough decisions, then you should get out of the way and let somebody else do it for you."

Public Service

"What I am is probably so corny that people just don't want to believe it.

"What I'm interested in is not anything secretive. It's called public service. I have a deep, abiding sense of obligation that makes it very hard for me to see the waste and the damage and the hurt that occur every day. I can't help wanting to do something about it. I feel so lucky to be married to Bill, because his being governor has made it natural for me to get involved. But you don't have to be married to a political man to do public service."

Several of her professors at Yale had been members of the JFK administration and the LBJ presidency:

"People like that helped symbolize the kind of public [and] private professional opportunities and obligations

69

that I was interested in. They went in and out of public service, and I really thought that was a good model, and they might have had very different points of view, but they used their education and their professional training to be of public benefit."

"If you have blessings, then you should feel some sense of obligation to share those with others."

"Balance is the key, and the elements of that balance are family, work and service . . ."

"I have a burning desire to do what I can, a desire to make the world around me—kind of going out in concentric circles—better for everybody."

"I really believe in service. I think it's the way you fully round out a life and learn about yourself and enter fully into the human condition. It comes from my religious beliefs and from my own personal experience. Being able to help people in small ways, as well as trying to make changes you believe will help large numbers of people, is very important to me. Being involved in health care reform, which I believe in passionately, is one of the most important things I could dream of having any role in. So that part has been very gratifying."

"I love my husband, and I love my country, and I can't imagine a better place to be than where I will be after January 20 [1992]. I want to make a difference."

MEDIA SCRUTINY

Asked how they deal with media scrutiny:

"Well, it has been a learning experience. That's what my mother used to say to me when I'd come home and had some disagreement on the playground. She'd say, 'Consider this a learning experience.' Well, it was more than we ever expected. And it was certainly more mean-spirited than we ever expected. And we had to work through that and get to a point where you can take criticism seriously but not personally. And try to—if there is something of legitimacy that someone is saying—try to learn from it, but also recognize that people will criticize you in public life for their own reasons, and they will make things up if they think it will promote their particular position. So take that also for what it is.

"I can't say that we've gotten to the point where it never bothers us, because, contrary to some opinion, you know, you do have your emotions still when you end up in positions like this, and it does hurt. But I think that both of us are very lucky that we have a supportive family and

71

lots of friends, and that we try to remember what's really important in our lives and not let this bother us."

Audience member's question on CBS This Morning: *"Living in the public spotlight like you do, I was just wondering how many times you thought of packing it all up and moving to a remote island."*

"Well, you know, I said the other day maybe the South Pole was looking more and more attractive. That does cross my mind from time to time, but it doesn't stay long, because I really think what my husband's doing is important."

Asked on Newshour with Jim Lehrer, *May 28, 1996, if she's keeping a diary:*

"Heavens no! It would get subpoenaed. I can't write anything down [laughing]."

"I told Chelsea one day that before it was over they'll attack me, they'll attack you, they'll attack your cat, they'll attack your goldfish."

"Maybe this time the candidate and the press will get it right. The public can learn enough to know whether a candidate is a decent person without having to pick you apart so much that there is nothing left at the end."

"It is very hard, when people lie about you and attack you, not to feel anger. If we act human, which is to say we resent it, we get angry about it—that somehow diminishes us."

About being called "the Hillary problem":

"I don't know how to feel about it. . . . I think I'll just have to be more . . . *careful* in the way I express my feelings, so I don't inadvertently hurt anybody."

"The press doesn't believe you have any feelings. They sure don't believe in the Bible."

"I have read enough history to know that no matter what I do, I will be fair game."

Criticism

"I learned a long time ago, because my husband has been in this business for so long, that unfair criticism goes with the territory."

"There are no guideposts, no signposts, to understand it. I think we're between generations in a very significant way, and change is always difficult, always going to be resisted. We have to figure out ways of making change into a friend, instead of an enemy. I've got *My Days*, Eleanor Roosevelt's newspaper columns, next to my bed because it's important for me to put this experience I'm going through into some kind of historical context."

"You can be very involved and on the front lines like Mrs. Roosevelt and be criticized. Or you can be totally concerned with your family and not venture forth and be criticized. It is a no-win situation."

"The harder they hit, the more encouraged I get."

Asked on Larry King Live, *May 5, 1994, "What do you make of the anger at you?"*

"Oh, I think some of it is part of the fear and insecurity about what my husband is trying to do and the direction he is trying to take our country and get us all moving together again. I think some of it is because I'm a kind of transition person in the history of our country."

"Meaning what?"

"Well, I think that, you know, for many women, the life that I've led, trying to balance family and work, is what we're all trying to work out in our own lives. But we've never had somebody in my position before who had done that. And I've, you know, worked most of my life, and I really believe in women having the full range of choices available to them. I don't care what choice they make, as long as they make the right choice for them. But I think some people would rather have stereotypes. It's easier that way."

"I personally do not believe that this level of paranoiac, conspiracy-driven investigation is appropriate—of anybody in public life, not just me. This is a matter that goes way beyond me. It is just *absurd*. If you take historical precedent, no president has ever had any of his activities before he became president investigated like this. And a lot of people came into office having made a lot of money, and with people knowing they made money through friends. We came in having lost money. We came in with very little in the way of resources. We are subjected to a whole new set of standards. We don't have a vacation house in Maine, we don't have a ranch in California, we don't have a cottage on the shore of Maryland—we don't have any of those things.

"So how many times do we have to say, over and over again, 'Look—we spent our lives primarily in public service.' Even my law practice was subordinated to our public service."

Speech at George Washington University:

"I had a friend of mine say to me the other day that she had the best Thanksgiving she ever had because her mother-in-law didn't come, and so she didn't . . . have herself criticized from the moment that, you know, the dinner was in the oven until it was cleaned up afterwards, and I thought to myself, 'That's sort of like the media.' I mean, it's like, you know, it's like your mother-in-law coming for Thanksgiving dinner."

To The Wall Street Journal:

"If someone has a female boss for the first time, maybe they can't take out their hostility on her, so they take it out on me."

"I don't mind criticism, and I don't mind controversy, as long as people are criticizing what is being done or said instead of personally attacking each other. I think that's an unfortunate by-product of our politics today where, instead of engaging each other on the merits of an issue and searching for common ground, people stand back and hurl insults at each other. That's not a very useful way for us to work together. So let's be willing to work together instead of staking out ideological positions and engaging in personal attacks. And then the controversy is fair game. That's what a democracy thrives on."

To Margaret Truman:

"I have no quarrel with anyone who wants to criticize the president or me. I know it comes with the territory. I often think of what your father went through. But it's difficult."

William Safire of the New York Times *said in a column that he didn't believe she was telling the truth:*

"Well, I don't take what Mr. Safire says very seriously. As you pointed out, I was working for the committee that impeached President Nixon, for whom Mr. Safire worked, and best I can tell is still working. In fact, my mother took some offense, because being called a 'congenital liar' seems to reflect badly on her and my late father."

"I don't even read what people mostly say about me. I figure that'll all wash out historically, and a lot of this kind of day-by-day stuff doesn't amount to very much. And, in fact, I look at each day's news and I think, 'What will be important in five years, or fifty years?' "

Asked to explain the level of animosity toward her:

"I apparently remind some people of their mother-in-law or their boss, or something."

The Tabloids

On a tabloid report that she was pregnant with an alien child:

"If the alien baby comes, we're ready and looking forward to it. I've always wanted a sibling for Chelsea."

"We've been hit with all kinds of accusations. The kinds of accusations that are in the tabloids next to the people with cow heads and the like."

"Good marriages are seldom celebrated, while every tiff or spat in a celebrity marriage becomes tabloid fodder."

78

Her Image, Her Self

SELF-IMAGE

"I have been trying to wear contact lenses since I was sixteen, but I could never get the hard lenses to stay in my eyes. I'm really nearsighted, so I had a choice—either try to wear hard contacts and not see or wear my glasses. So, obviously, I wore my glasses."

In 1987:

"I think being the spouse of a governor, I have to look good."

In 1993:

"I've never thought about clothes so much in my life!"

"I've never put this much focus on my image—*never*!"

In 1995:

"I don't get this whole image-creation thing."

About her image (1993):

"I'm a Rorschach test."

"I don't vest my identity in my hair or my clothes. I view that just as what you have to do to get up in the morning and go out in the world."

"What I have learned is you have got to give people a chance to know you. People may be glad to see you, but they are initially standoffish, waiting to find out who you are. Well, Bill and I just moved into America's neighborhood. I want them to know as much about me and all my different roles as possible."

"I don't see how I could change who I am because of the position I'm in. I actually think that in the long run if people have some better idea about you, it may be controversial, but at least they know where you stand."

"I was really one of the people in America who could always look back and say, you know, the meritocracy really is alive and well, because I was given so many opportunities."

"I'm not a behind-the-scenes kind of person. I'm very overt."

Barbara Walters (ABC News 20/20, January 12, 1996): "Do you have a terrible temper?"

"No, but I do get angry about things. I'm not going to deny that. I do—there are things that I think are wrong or things that I think should be fixed, and I am not at all shy about expressing my opinion. I try to be a direct person and—but I don't tell people what to do. I say, 'Here's what I think and I'm concerned about this.' "

She sees herself as . . .

" . . . a working mother trying to balance all these responsibilities, very much like those that are faced in millions of American homes."

Asked if she thinks of herself as intimidating:

"I didn't until I kept reading that I was. And so I said, 'Well, maybe I am.' "

"I'm not one of these Energizer bunnies."

Katie Couric: "Millions of people see you as a role model and millions of other people see you as a very threatening person. Why do you think you are such a lightning rod?"

"Because I think women's roles right now are lightning rods every day in so many different ways. In workplaces and kitchens, and places all over America, people are struggling to define what it means to be a woman, a mother, a wife—all of the different roles that we play. And because my husband is the first of our generation to be elected president, it's the first time that a lot of those private discussions have really been played out at such a very high and visible point in our public life."

She'd like people to look at her . . .

" . . . and say, you know, what really matters is that for twenty-five years she's cared about kids and that's been a consistent theme, and maybe I should learn about that, instead of, 'Omigosh, she's changed her hairdo again.' "

"I think you have to be true to yourself. You have to find your own voice."

HUMOR

A White House guest is speaking on the phone to his wife. The first lady takes the receiver and jokes:

"Don't worry, now, we've worked out a way for him to pay for the Ming vase he knocked over."

Speech at the Joint Armed Forces Wives' Luncheon, November 19, 1993:

"This has been so much fun. I don't usually get to say that when I go to events.

"I am very grateful for the invitation to be here, and I have certainly enjoyed my visits at lunch with a number of you, particularly at my table and in the rest room."

Katie Couric: "What about the comparisons to Lady Macbeth? Do you think it's because you're a powerful woman—where does that come from?"

"Oh, I think some writer somewhere thinks it makes a good line and he's more likely to get his piece in print."

Couric: "You don't walk around the White House saying, 'Out, damned spot?' "

"No, only when I'm trying to wash something."

Speech at the University of Arkansas in Fayetteville:

"Stand up against the easy answers, the stereotypes, the labels. You know the kind of thing I'm talking about:

"If you're under twenty-five, you're an apathetic generation X-er. If you're over forty, you're a self-indulgent baby boomer.

"If you're a liberal, you're a bleeding heart. If you're a conservative, you have no heart.

"If you're a Democratic president from Arkansas, you're accused of being all of the above.

"And if you're the wife of a Democratic president from Arkansas, you have to worry about your hair a lot."

FASHION

"I just wear what I like and what strikes my fancy at the time. That's always been a character defect of mine. I've never been able to do trunk shows, because I can't think that far ahead."

Asked how she felt about being a fashion role model:
"It's a hoot."

"I didn't have a makeover. I just changed my hair and have gotten more diligent in the last several years about exercising and all the things we are supposed to do as we get older."

HAIRDOS (AND DON'TS)

"Anyone who's looked at pictures of me, going back to when I was in high school, knows I change my hair all the time. I did that long before I was in the public eye. I try different types of clothes. I don't take it seriously . . . I think it's fun."

"I guess I don't have the right genes for managing my hair without a headband when I'm traveling."

On her constantly changing hairstyles:
"Now, this, as my husband says, is one of his favorite hairstyles, because it is what I wore in high school. I didn't

know him in high school, but he has my graduation picture. It's always been one of his favorite pictures, and the other day he said, 'Oh, this is wonderful—you're back to your high school hair.'

"Hair to me has always been the one part of my body that I had control over. I could not grow any taller, I could not lengthen my legs, I could not make my eyes have perfect vision—there was nothing else I could really do. But my hair has always been a source of great amusement to me. I've cut it, permed it, highlighted it, worn it short, worn it long. I was always having fun with it, and I never realized it would be such a serious subject. I mean, do you wear the same clothes every year? Even if you think you've got your style down pat, you still want some slight variation. Accessorize it, do something with it—well, that's the way I feel about my hair."

Asked on Larry King Live, *May 5, 1994: "Okay, Hillary, the key question is, what's with the hair?"*

"What is today's called? It's called spray it and hope it doesn't fall in your face when you're talking to Larry."

"Who does it?"

"Oh, I have great help with my hair, yes, and I need help.

"Ever since I was a little girl, Larry. Yeah, it's been something I've struggled with all my life. I'm hoping somebody is going to form a group, Hair Anonymous, that I could join."

"And have secret meetings and stand up."

"Secret meetings and you stand up and talk about your bad hair days."

In a 1993 speech at the University of Texas in Austin she noted that Ann Richards and she were wearing similar outfits:

"I suppose the only thing left for me is to get a hairdo like that. You know, I'm actually due for a new one, and I figure that if we ever want to get Bosnia off the front page all I have to do is either put on a headband or change my hair and we'll be occupied with something else."

About her new short haircut (1993):

"When the president called for sacrifice, I decided on a 50 percent cut."

"I like to experiment with my hair. I mean, I don't even know what it's going to look like this time next year. I just think you should have some fun with your life and not take yourself real seriously."

RELIGION

"And in nearly every religion that I am aware of, there is a variation of the Golden Rule. And even for the nonreligious, it is a tenet of people who believe in humanistic principles."

Remarks at a National Prayer Luncheon, February 2, 1995:

"The last time I spoke in public about spirituality, around the time of my father's death, I was astonished to realize that there were many people for whom spirituality should be confined to events like this, and not brought out into the public arena. I was amused when one commentator wrote that my critics were divided between conservatives who suspect I did not mean what I said and liberals who feared that I did.

"And I have become accustomed over the past year to living between those kinds of poles and trying as best I can to navigate what is for many of us uncharted terrain. Because as my husband said this morning, freedom of religion does not mean, and should not mean, freedom from religion. And striking the appropriate balance, and being able to witness in a public role what one feels and lives through one's own spiritual journey, opens one up to misunderstanding and criticism."

"The very core of what I believe is this concept of individual worth, which I think flows from all of us being creatures of God and being imbued with a spirit."

"The secular press doesn't know how to talk about religion except in stereotypes."

"Wisdom. When I went to Sunday school years ago our books often talked about how Jesus grew in wisdom and stature. I think about that often because it is unlikely I will grow any further in stature, but I certainly hope I will grow more in wisdom as the years go by."

"I have always believed that Christ wanted us to be joyous, to look at the face of Creation and to know that there was more joy than any of us could imagine. Or as Mother Teresa told us this morning, to see the joy on the face of a homeless beggar, who is picked up off the street and brought in to die, and says joyously, 'Thank you.'"

On Live with Regis & Kathie Lee, *June 10, 1996:*

"You have to fight this feeling of hopelessness and helplessness in your own life as well as in the lives of people around you. . . . I'm blessed with the kind of religious faith and upbringing that has given me a lot that I can fall back on. I have a supportive husband and a wonderful child myself, so that I see the blessings that I have been given, and I think to myself that there are a lot of people out there who just weren't as lucky as I was. Not that it's better or worse. There are a lot of really decent people who have a terrible, terrible, tough time."

Asked if she believes in intercessory prayer:

"I do. I do. And not only do I believe in it, I think there is increasing evidence of it. There is an interesting hospital study in which patients of comparable medical condition were prayed for, and prayers were, apparently, the only difference that could be discovered between how the patients were treated."

"I have a lot of special prayers, and you know I rely on those in my daily life. I sure do.

"I carry a lot of them with me, but it's not something I really talk about. Except I would say this: There is just a real opportunity for people, through regular prayer and contemplation or just taking a few minutes out to think about themselves, to gain strength. And if it becomes a habit, it's always there for you. And I just hope more people, whatever their religious faith or spiritual beliefs might be, would try that. It can provide a great source of strength."

"I think that prayer and faith are the province of the family, and I believe that what we ought to be trying to figure out how to do is to get prayer back in the family."

The White House Years

THE WHITE HOUSE ITSELF

"There is a wonderful feeling to this house because when you think that this is the corridor that, you know, Thomas Jefferson walked up and down and that Abraham Lincoln walked up and down—it used to be that this was a business corridor. There were bedrooms here as well. But much of the business of the White House went on here before President Theodore Roosevelt built the West Wing, so that, for example, you would have many office seekers and government officials, perhaps, crowded up at this end of the hallway waiting for President Lincoln. And he would then have them coming in to meet with him over and over again."

"There's a special warehouse for all of the furnishings that belong here in the White House, and everything is cataloged and kept so well. It's . . . part of the responsibility of the National Park Service to assist the White House in caring for this house, so they run that for us."

"I really love this house, and I love the idea that not only the presidents and their families but literally millions and millions of Americans have walked these halls and come to receptions and taken a tour. You know, it's the only house of a head of state anywhere in the world that's open to the public. You can't go to any other country and have the accessibility to this kind of a place except here in America."

Asked if she feels at home there:

"I do. It is so overwhelming to live in this house, because there's so much history. And it is a living museum. But it's also our home, and we try to make it feel like our home."

"We have a lot of artwork that was formerly in storage now on display in the White House, and we are in the process of making sure we have somewhere depicted every president and first lady who ever lived here, so that we have some kind of memory of their presence."

"I have this little kitchen upstairs. It's this kitchen that is ours, where we have things in our refrigerator, like apples that I can peel and make applesauce with."

In the newly refurbished Blue Room:

"My one hope was that we could create a more blue feeling in the room but not make it so blue that it would be dark and shrink the room, especially at night. At night in this room, with its view looking out at the Washington Monument and the Jefferson Memorial across the fountain, there is a sense of magic and beauty unmatched."

LIFE IN THE WHITE HOUSE

Tom Brokaw (NBC News at Sunrise, January 18, 1993): "What do you think you'll do the first morning that you awaken in the White House and look at each other?"

"Pull the covers over our heads."

Three weeks after moving into the White House, Mrs. Clinton and Chelsea went shopping at a Washington, D.C., supermarket:

"I wanted to stock the second-floor kitchen so the people who work there could see the kinds of thing we like to eat. I picked up Chelsea at school, and we stopped at the first supermarket we saw. I opened my wallet and discovered that I had only eleven dollars. I asked the manager if the store took credit cards. He was just so stunned to see me that he became speechless. I had to keep saying, 'Do you take credit cards here?' Finally, he sort of stammered out that they didn't yet, but they were going to, and it would be soon, 'like March.' And I said, 'This is, like February, so I guess I can't buy anything today.'"

"There isn't really any way to prepare for it . . . when you walk in that door at the White House the day that your husband is inaugurated, you really do not know what you are walking into. You can read history, you can know that there are all kinds of experiences that people have had to go through, but until you actually are there, day in and day out, neither the wonder and the thrill and the excitement of it nor the challenges of it seem quite real. And it's a constant adjustment. And I think it's been an extraordinary and for me it's been a very positive and wonderful experience, but I could never have predicted how I would have reacted to what would have happened to me."

"I think it is a very quick and immersing experience to find yourself the subject of so many peoples' expectations while you're still trying to find out where the bathrooms are in the White House."

Asked about drawbacks to living in the White House:

"Well, the loss of privacy and, maybe even more than that, the loss of mobility are big drawbacks. I mean, I've had a chance a few times since we've been here to, you know, just put on some old clothes and go for a couple of long walks, but you don't feel free to come and go, like I always did before. And my husband, particularly, is really restricted from doing that. So that's hard because, you know, you don't want this office to interfere with your understanding of what's going on in the country and what's real to people."

"I told Bill we have a budget deficit, an investment deficit and a sleep deficit. I believe, with Churchill, that naps are a restorative."

"The worst part is the lack of privacy and the inability to move easily, to do the things that we took for granted. I used to get in the car with Chelsea every Saturday and take her to ballet, and then I'd pick her up and we'd go to lunch and run errands, go grocery shopping. I really miss the kind of time that you need with your child—just pushing a cart up and down a grocery lane, just walking. We have to work at finding those times together."

"I like to know what my next week is going to look like. Then I always like to know a day or two in advance what a specific day is going to look like in terms of my public obligations. And then I try to carve out big chunks of time to be with my daughter or to have a dinner with friends or just to have some time to relax. And I really do try to organize my time so that it gives me what I need, which is, yes, time to try to get whatever work I have done. But time to just decompress and kick back."

Asked if she spends as much time with her husband as before:

"I see him maybe a little bit more, because I'm not off at my law office. Chelsea was off on a school trip, so Bill and I decided to have dinner outside on the Truman Balcony. All the cares of the day—I could just feel them ebbing away, sitting out there looking at the beautiful spring. The air is so soft. Everything is blooming. Bill and I have just been wandering around here in this dazed spring fever."

Asked about the movie theater—if that's their best perk:

"Oh, yeah, the movie theater. The movie theater and Camp David. We spent Thanksgiving at Camp David and really loved it."

"If you don't stay in touch with the daily routine that most lives are made up of, it's really easy to forget what the texture of life truly is, what it's like for other people. And that's something I worry about a lot in the White House. I think that it's been a great loss to our country that we have so isolated our presidents and their families."

"I frankly have gotten a little frustrated and itchy being in the White House because I feel cut off from people, and I feel that I'm not really out there doing what I care about and making a contribution. I've always been very involved in any community I've ever lived in. I've actually been trying to think about how I could be better integrated into my community, which is Washington now."

Asked what she doesn't like about the job:

"It's hard being so confined. You know, feeling that you can't just walk out the door and go to the store. You know, I was over in a Safeway store the other day, and I was there to promote health care benefits. But I loved being in the store. I haven't been in a store since I came to Washington, except one, you know, little effort that didn't pan out."

On life at the White House:

"One of the primary goals I had was to make sure that my husband and my daughter felt at home, because although this is the people's house and it's a museum and it's a great place where wonderful matters of state occur, it is our home."

"I know that we have had some funny experiences in the past three or so years, where, you know, my husband will say, 'Gee, I want a banana,' and next thing you know there are bananas everywhere. So, you know, we have learned to be, you know, maybe a little bit more careful about that."

Asked in 1996 if she had it to do over again, knowing what she knows now, would she do it:

"Absolutely. I wake up every day just wondering about what's going to happen next."

Holiday Time

"None of the holiday celebrations would be possible without the volunteers who come from as far away as California to help tie burgundy and gold bows, make wreaths, string lights and garlands and hang ornaments for the thirty trees scattered throughout the White House complex. (We have our own tree in the private quarters on the second floor and, thanks to some cat-loving volunteers, a special Socks tree on the third floor.)"

"We go pretty far to celebrate every major holiday. Bill goes crazy hiding Easter eggs. He always finds great places. Now, he'll have more rooms to torment us in."

For Christmas 1992, they adopt a needy family . . .

". . . which we personally take responsibility for. We get things they need and deliver them, usually on Christmas Eve. We started doing that with Chelsea a long time ago. And we also try to go by some of the shelters in town and visit with the people there and try to give them some things that are real Christmassy—especially the children, but the adults as well. And we go to church on Christmas Eve as well as Christmas Day. Christmas is really important to us."

Talking on Larry King Live, *December 24, 1994:*

"Everything about Christmas is exciting to my family. We love the carols, we love the traditions, we love all the Christmas foods and all the baking, which we personally do, as well as what's done here in the White House. We love the entertaining. We like everything about it."

On Larry King Live, *December 23, 1995:*

"Christmas is a time when we're supposed to not only think about our blessings but also about what it means to be a peacemaker. And certainly, this past year, the United States and the president have shown what it takes to make peace in lots of places in the world. It's not easy. It's not sure. But we're not guaranteed that. But what we have to do is keep trying."

"You know, the Christmas story is a story of hope and love and possibility for everyone. And all of us need that. I mean, everyone's life can be touched and transformed by the Christmas story. And, I hope that, in this season, people will stop and think about how they can bring more love into their own lives and into the lives of people around them. And I hope they will also stop for a minute and maybe put themselves in the shoes of another person and think about how they can further goodwill and peace by being more understanding of each other."

Showing off the 1994 Christmas card:

"Have you all seen the Christmas card for this year? . . . Over here you have a saxophone under the tree. There is Socks, who actually supervised much of the decorating of last weekend. This [a gingerbread house] is modeled on the president's boyhood home, and it has a marvelous vision of the German shepherd, King. My husband and his family had a series of German shepherds, all of whom were named King."

"One of the things that the president and Chelsea and I like to do is that at the end of every event—and we have events every single day for the rest of the Christmas season—when everybody's gone, we come back downstairs, and we walk around, and we spend a lot of time in front of the tree in different places because you can literally look at this tree for hours and keep discovering something new."

Interviewed just before Christmas 1995, when she was not wearing the famous necklace of blinking bulbs:

"The staff always worries about what I'm going to turn up in—antlers, flashing bulbs. I can't find the necklace, but if I do, you'll see it."

"There was one party, and I'm trying to remember which president it was, but they actually imported snow inside the East Room so the children could have a snowball fight. Teddy Roosevelt is just famous for this house being wide open to his children and their pets. You know, they had a little pony they used to take up and down the elevator because the elevator was a relatively recent addition. So they kept the pony out in the back, but they would bring him in the house, the children would, and he'd go up and down with them. You know, there was always a New Year's Day reception until Herbert Hoover, and that was cut off. But for more than 100 years, people would line up and they could all come in to see the president."

"One of the things I never thought I'd say is that I miss shopping during Christmas."

White House Cuisine

"I like all kinds of cuisines, but I want the White House to be especially noted for its American cuisine. And we are also looking at trying to make everything the White House serves healthier, since I'm on my health care kick."

On changes in White House cuisine:

"We are trying to move toward healthy, fresh American food."

"The good news is that my husband is the most easily satisfied when it comes to cooking. The bad news is he loves to eat even when things are not always right for him."

"We are big broccoli eaters. You know, he gets an unfair rap. An occasional trip to a fast-food restaurant is not the worst of all possible sins."

She told Tom Brokaw of her plans to change the president's diet:

"We've made a lot of progress on, you know, pasta and things like that, but tofu has been hard for us. . . . We're keeping at it till we find something we like."

BEING FIRST LADY

Asked what is a first lady:

"A partner. A partner who represents for all of us a view of who her husband is, as well as a symbol of women's concerns and interests at a particular time."

On the term "first lady":

"I don't use it much personally, but I don't object to people using it because it is a tradition that we think started with Martha Washington. So, it's not the term so much, it's the expectations that surround the role that I find fascinating. I have spent a lot of time in the last several years reading about my predecessors, and have discovered that nearly every one of them had a kind of bumpy time here because there's really no way to satisfy the extraordinary expectations that are put upon the person who is married to the president. And it has been both somewhat sustained, if you will, as well as a cautionary tale to realize that the women who have been here before have encountered many different kinds of challenges. And at the end of the day, you have to be yourself, you have to say and stand for what you believe in, you have to be willing to get up and go ahead and take the slings and arrows and just try to persist through them, because it's apparently an inevitable part of our American democracy.''

Keynote address at Scripps College, April 26, 1994:

"I'm often asked if what I am doing in Washington creates a new role model for first ladies. And I always say I don't want to create any new stereotype. I want to free women to live according to their own needs and desires. I do not want to create a new category that anyone after me must somehow fit into. I want all women to be given the respect they deserve to have for the choices they may make.''

"I don't think you can get used to it. I think what you do, as Eleanor Roosevelt—who is one of my great heroines—said, you know, you just grow as thick a skin as you possibly can and you try to take criticism seriously but not personally. But sometimes that is difficult, especially for people who have had a whole life and a whole career where they have been lauded and successful all of a sudden to get into this arena, where the rules really are different than they are anywhere else. And to be criticized for the first time. I think unless you've had some getting used to it, it could be devastating.''

Asked in 1995 to name her most pleasurable moments as first lady so far:

"The passage of the Brady Bill. And the ban on assault weapons."

Asked in 1993 what she'd like to say about her work as first lady four years hence:

"I'd like to be able to point to *real* progress. I'd like to be able to say there are fewer children in poverty, fewer children going without health care and missing immunizations."

FORMER FIRST LADIES

"As I have learned this past fifteen months, there is no prescription or role model or cookbook for being first lady. And if you look back at the lives of Martha Washington or Abigail Adams or Dolley Madison or Edith Wilson or Eleanor Roosevelt or Bess Truman or Mamie Eisenhower, you can see that each woman has defined the role in a way that is true to herself, how she can help her husband, take care of her family, make her contribution to our nation."

"I've learned that each one has tried to do what she thought was best for her husband and her family and the country as she saw her obligations. And that almost without exception, every one was criticized for something by somebody. If you lived your life trying to make sure that nobody ever criticized you, you would probably never get out of bed—and then you'd be criticized for that."

Asked by a caller on Larry King Live, *May 5, 1994, if she is in touch with former first ladies:*

"I've had a really wonderful experience in the times that I've had to talk to the former first ladies. I've had a chance to visit with Lady Bird Johnson, who I think is one of the great women of our country, and of our times, who has given me advice and encouragement. Rosalynn Carter and Betty Ford have both been stalwart supporters of health care reform, particularly mental health reform. And they have shared with me on occasion some of the challenges they faced when they were attempting to bring about changes, when they found themselves in the position I'm in. I've also had wonderful conversations with Mrs. Onassis, Jackie Kennedy Onassis, whom I admire greatly, and whom I've talked with about how she protected her children and what she did to give them a normal life. And I've also enjoyed very much my conversations with Mrs. Reagan and Mrs. Bush. Both have been personally very supportive and kind to me. So, you ask a good question. And I wish there were even more opportunities for me to visit with these women, because I admire and respect them."

"I have recollections of extraordinary policy roles taken by Eleanor Roosevelt and very strong positions on the environment by Lady Bird Johnson."

"I admire greatly Betty Ford's personal bravery and outspokenness on women's issues—particularly on the ERA and breast cancer—when it was not at all easy. I think President and Mrs. Carter both made great contributions on a lot of the difficult issues that confronted the country. And I think Mrs. Carter's work on behalf of mental health and President Carter's continuing example after he left the White House are a great legacy."

Martha Washington

"She was referred to as 'Lady Washington,' and they thought she was putting on airs and acting much too regally. And every single woman who has been in that position has been criticized in some way or another, almost regardless of what she has chosen to do."

Campaigning in Denver, Representative Patricia Schroeder introduced Hillary Rodham Clinton, pointing out that those who criticized the president's wife should remember Martha Washington, who camped out with George for three winters to try to rally the Revolutionary Army. Nevertheless, she was criticized for wearing cotton instead of silk, for speaking English instead

107

of the more fashionable French, and for other reasons. When Mrs. Clinton took the podium she laughed and said:

"You left out the most important part—when Martha Washington was pilloried by the press corps for wearing headbands at Valley Forge."

Eleanor Roosevelt

Keynote address at the dedication of the Eleanor Roosevelt College, January 26, 1995:

"I am a die-hard Eleanor Roosevelt fan. I have read her autobiography, her newspaper columns, and many books about her and President Roosevelt. And from the first time I can remember hearing about her, I have always admired her."

"She was often attacked and criticized, but there was never any confusion in her own mind about what constituted a meaningful life. She refused to be categorized or stereotyped, which, of course, greatly frustrated her critics. She was one of those rare people who strike that elusive balance between 'me' and 'we.' Between our rights and expectations as individuals and our obligations to the larger community. She considered herself as a citizen. Someone who was there trying to make sure that democracy worked well. Someone who wanted to help educate other citizens about what they could do."

"It's a real honor for me to be ever compared to Eleanor Roosevelt, whom I think made tremendous contributions to this country in very tough times. And I think all of the women who have been in that position have tried in their own ways to figure out how to balance their responsibilities to themselves and to their husbands and families, and to the country. And I think that's what I'm trying to figure out how to do. I bring a different perspective. I'm of a different generation, in many respects. And I'm trying to determine, you know, how to keep all the roles in balance and make the contribution I would like to make."

In his book The Choice, *Bob Woodward reveals her imaginary conversations with Eleanor Roosevelt:*

"I try to figure out what she would do in my shoes. She usually responds by telling me to buck up or at least to grow skin as thick as a rhinoceros."

Speaking about her imaginary conversations with Eleanor Roosevelt, at a Nashville conference on families:

"Shortly before I arrived, I had one of my conversations with Mrs. Roosevelt and she thinks this is a terrific idea as well."

Jacqueline Kennedy Onassis

"Oh, I just am crazy about her. And she talked about raising children, because I think she's done such a magnificent job with her children under the most extraordinary of circumstances probably anybody's had to face in our lifetime. And she talked about how it's so important to, you know, to give your children responsibility, give them as normal a life as you can despite everything that's going on around them. Don't let them have too much attention, or be exposed too much, because they deserve a chance to grow up to be who they're going to be."

After Jacqueline Kennedy Onassis had died:

"She was a great support to me personally when I started talking with her in the summer of 1992 about the challenges and opportunities of being in this position and how she had managed so well to carve out the space and privacy that children need to grow into what they have a right to become. She will always be more than a great first lady. She was a great woman and a great friend."

Barbara Bush

"I don't think we ought to move from one stereotype of a first lady to another. I admire Barbara Bush and all the women who have found themselves in that position, who have tried to shape the position to their needs and their husbands' needs. The choices a woman makes should be respected."

Diane Sawyer (ABC News, January 14, 1993): "Did Mrs. Bush give you any advice about all of this?"

"Oh, she said that I would love living in the White House because the people who were there were so wonderful and wanting to make that house, which is America's house, just the very best place it could be. And she said, 'Have some fun.' You know, she was just so gracious about it. I really enjoyed my time with her, but I've always liked her and had a good time with her."

Foreign Policy

"I think many people in the United States are mistaken about how much money we spend on foreign aid. We spend about 1 percent, and many people believe we spend 20 or 25 percent. And so I'd like, first of all, for Americans to know that that 1 percent investment really has made a difference in helping to solve problems but also in helping America to be stronger by solving problems around the world. And the second thing I would like Americans to know is that we sometimes, through the work that we do in other countries, learn lessons that we can bring back home. The United States has always been a leader. I want us to continue to be a leader, and I don't think you lead from behind walls. I don't think you lead by walking away from the world. I think you lead by remaining engaged and trying to shape events."

At a ceremony honoring nongovernmental organizations' relief efforts in the former Yugoslavia:

"I hope you saw the World Vision exhibit of drawings and photographs by Bosnian children that is on display downstairs. These pictures are at once remarkable and heartbreaking. To see the conflict through children's eyes reminds us that children bear a special burden in war; not only are they robbed of their loved ones, of their homes and schools and communities, they are robbed of their spirit. Today, the children of Bosnia are truly the world's orphans."

ENTERTAINING

On the visit of the emperor and empress of Japan:

"Friendship among nations is built on many things, including an appreciation of beauty and culture and art. Every spring, nature reminds us of that friendship in the bloom of cherry blossoms transplanted from Japan so many years ago. The emperor and empress told us that they themselves performed a similar transplant many years ago, taking the seeds from a white birch tree at the Blair House where they were staying across the street from this White House and planting them at home in the Imperial Palace gardens, where four decades later a white birch tree grows straight and strong."

Speaking to Regis Philbin and Kathie Lee Gifford about a dinner planned for French President Jacques Chirac:

"This is the most nervewracking state dinner we've had. . . . It's a little bit special because the French are so famous for their cuisine and they have such high standards."

The Clintons invited Michael Douglas, who starred in The American President *as a widowed president, to the state dinner for French President Chirac:*

"I thought he might want to come to a real state dinner."

"One of my husband's real problems with being president is that he really likes going out. But it's not as easy just to pick up and go. So we try to compensate for it by having lots of people in. And we have entertained hundred and hundreds of people. Maybe we're into the thousands. All kinds of people—old friends who come to stay the night, college friends of his and mine. We also have lots of people who will come by sixish or so for a drink or a visit."

WORLD TRAVELS

"Traveling as first family means traveling heavy. We can't go anywhere without dozens of staff and security people. And it's hard to sneak in and out of town on Air Force One."

Berlin

During an appearance in Berlin:

"Today, the enemy wears many masks—the mask of ethnic hatred, the mask of racial hatred, the mask of religious hatred. Today, hostility and aggression are much less organized and can burst onto the scene at a moment's notice."

Poland

On a 1996 visit to Auschwitz:

"The lessons of this place should never be forgotten. . . . You can't even let up for a minute . . . "

South Asia

Remarks at the Alice Deal Junior High School (Washington, D.C.) Promotional Exercises, June 9, 1995:

"I hope that you will count your blessings about being an

114

American at this point in our country's history. I was in South Asia just a few weeks ago with my daughter. And we saw things and met people that just opened our eyes. It is humbling, I must say, to shake the hands of men and women who are attempting to lead their countries into more democratic and prosperous futures; who have lost mothers, fathers, and brothers and sons to assassination, who themselves have been exiled and imprisoned and tortured because they wanted to live more like we live.

"They wanted the ideals and the vision of what this country stands for. Now, have we always fulfilled our own ideals and visions? Of course not. Do we always have to continue to examine where we are and where we're going and try to do a better job? Yes, we do. But the truth is that there has never been a society in our history or at the present time that has tried harder to do what had never been done before to provide opportunity to all people and bring all people together in some common purpose on behalf of our country."

Remarks to the UN Development Fund for Women's "Women's Economic Empowerment Zone" Panel, September 6, 1995:

"From the Grameen Bank in Bangladesh or to the Self-employed Women's Association in India, or to the work in Ghana that you will hear about, to banks and programs modeled on these from Indonesia to the Dominican Republic, to my own country, we have seen that microlending works. Women who have received loans from the Grameen Bank, for example, have a repayment rate of 97 percent, and often within one year. And they invest their money well.

"Some buy milk cows to expand their families' agricultural livestock; some buy materials to make handicrafts which they then sell. Others make bricks or repair bicycles. But the fact is: Give a woman a seed, and she will plant it, she will water it, nurture it, then reap it, share its fruits, and finally, she will replant it. In this way, step by step, the world's poorest women are leading their families, their communities and their countries to a better future. When we help these women to sow, we all reap."

"Because of the success of such programs, the World Bank, and USAID, along with eight other major donors, have joined together to form the consultative group to aid the poor in order to finance small loans to the world's poor, the vast majority of whom are female. This is the kind of joint effort that we need to support."

"During my trip to South Asia, I saw example after example of women struggling to overcome poverty, illiteracy, inadequate health care and long-standing forms of discrimination. I saw poor and illiterate women who had organized around their capacity to borrow and save money, and were beginning to lift themselves and their families out of acute poverty. I saw women who had acquired skills to make crafts they could sell for profit. I saw women insisting that their daughters be given the same opportunities for schooling as their sons."

Ireland and Northern Ireland

She speaks of meeting with women in Belfast who had been working to unite people across the religious divide:

"One of the women said she considered herself a 'family feminist.' I loved that phrase, because I believe that, if you are a human being, one of your highest responsibilities is to the next generation. I mean, I have fought all my life for women to have the right to make the decisions that are best for them, and for me that included getting married, having a child."

"No matter how different we may be superficially, whatever religion we follow, whatever shade of color our skin might be, whatever our ethnic background, there is so much more that unites us than divides us, and if women begin talking with one another around kitchen tables, in cafés, in workplaces, we will discover that sense of shared identity."

"Women were—and are—a driving force behind peace in Northern Ireland."

"As we landed here, I felt as though I had been here before, although this is my very first trip to Ireland. I don't suppose one can grow up in America without knowing so many Irish Americans and without appreciating the many contributions that this culture has made to our own, and we are particularly reminded of our close ties this year, because you are observing the one hundred and fiftieth anniversary of the Great Famine. We know something of our own history because of the tragedy of yours.

"And being here today and having come from Northern Ireland yesterday, I understand even more clearly the ways in which Ireland has influenced American society, and I am learning more every minute about the way Irish women have influenced American society and still are today."

On a visit to Belfast, Northern Ireland:

"As the Lord Mayor said, in a moment the Christmas tree will be lit, as Christmas trees will be lit all over the world in the days to come. This Christmas, let us remember the reason behind why we light Christmas trees. Let us remember the reason for this great holiday celebration. And let us remember that we seek peace most of all for our children. May this be one of many, many happy and peaceful Christmases in Northern Ireland this year and for many years to come. And may God keep you, and bless you, and hold all of you in the palm of his hand."

The Former Yugoslavia

At a ceremony honoring nongovernmental organizations' relief efforts in the former Yugoslavia:

"We all know that a permanent peace will not come easily

to a place where neighbors have turned against neighbors and hatreds among different groups have undermined the larger Bosnian community. The war claimed thousands of lives, and countless people have been brutally victimized because of their ancestry and religion. Like children, women have endured particularly tragic consequences of the conflict in Bosnia."

"I am pleased to announce that through the United States Agency for International Development and the State Department's Bureau of Population, Refugees and Migration, the United States will support a new relief initiative in Bosnia focusing on families and children. Our partners in this effort will be the Catholic Relief Services and the International Orthodox Christian Charities. This marks the first time these two important groups have embarked on a project together. Their participation, along with church groups, Islamic associations, local nongovernmental organizations and professional associations is a crucial step in promoting religious reconciliation in Bosnia. The religious charities are committed to providing relief not simply to one religious group or another, not to one community or another, but to all people in Bosnia who need assistance. It is this kind of courageous cooperation that must be emulated throughout the region if peace is to hold."

"There is probably no other people in the world—and maybe in the history of the world—better equipped than Americans to help bring this kind of support and relief;

Americans coming from so many different backgrounds, races, ethnicities, religions, coming together as we do every day, to work here; and now doing it, as we are, throughout the world; trying to be peacemakers and to demonstrate how the barriers that divide us can be transcended."

FRIENDS AND FAMILY

Friends

"You have to have made your friends before now."

"I regret, for example, that I haven't had as much time to socialize or spend with friends. I don't get out a lot in Washington and I didn't get out a lot in Little Rock, because when I have time that is not spent on my work and my public activities, I want to be with my family. I think *that's* one of the reasons people say, 'Well, who is she? We don't know her.' I don't get out as much as many people do, because these years of child rearing go by so fast—I mean, Chelsea's going to be gone. I can go to dinner parties from now to kingdom come when she's in college and when she's grown up."

On New Age writer Marianne Williamson, after an article in Esquire *had reported that they were frequent lunch companions:*

"[Williamson] is neither my guru nor my spiritual adviser. She is a political supporter who has an intriguing view about popular culture."

"It's really important to us to have our friends and our families. It's really important to Chelsea, too, to be with familiar people that knew us before we lived here."

"One of the things that I have given up completely is time with friends and social time. We talk on the phone or try to see each other on special occasions. But I couldn't keep an active social life and do everything else."

Family

Bill Clinton

Asked during the 1992 campaign about Clinton's "character problems":

"When Americans get to know him the way the people of Arkansas know him, they'll understand that he doesn't have character problems. He's been elected five times."

"I'm amused when people think that because Bill is southern and a nice person and doesn't like to pick a fight, that he just likes to get along. Those people weren't there when he was picketed by the far right because we were setting up health clinics."

"I find I get very nervous when he does something like a debate or makes a major speech. Because, you know, my heart's in my throat and I want him to do well, and it's really hard on me."

"We care about the same issues and values and concerns. We are a partnership."

"What he's really done for me is share his heart—which is enormous. He is an incredibly loving and compassionate and caring person. And it has made me a better person. He has the most extraordinary amount of patience and love for people of all kinds, and it is almost unfailing. I have watched that ever since I first met him and marveled at it. It has been a standard by which I have judged my own ability to reach out and care and grow."

"He's also genuinely optimistic and enthusiastic about life. He is somebody who sees the glass as half full. He cares about every day—he wants to jam-pack it with more than the day can hold. It's maddening to try to keep him on any kind of schedule because he wants to listen to everybody. It's not that he doesn't want to go on to the next event; it's just that he doesn't want to leave where he is until he's had a chance to see everybody there."

Bill Clinton . . .

" . . . viewed his father's death as so irrational—so out of the blue—that it really did set a tone for his own sense of mortality. . . . Not just in his political career. It was reading everything he could read, talking to everybody he could talk to, staying up all night, because life was passing him by.

"I mean, it was . . . it was an intense sense of . . . what he might miss at any moment."

She recalls a legal seminar they went to:

"The fellow was showing us a problem on the screen, and it was a pretty hard problem and Bill was asleep. Well, I wasn't going to wake him up. It was a little embarrassing, but the lights were off, so I didn't think anybody would know he was sleeping. And the fellow was asking about the answer to this problem. None of us were really catching on. Bill woke up, answered the problem, and fell back asleep."

"He'll be watching some obscure basketball game, and he'll be reading and talking on the phone all at the same time and knowing exactly what is going on in each situation. If you stopped him and said 'What's the score?' he'd tell you. If you stopped him and said, 'What did the person you were talking to just say?' he'd repeat it verbatim, and if you stopped him and said, 'What did you just read?' he'd say what he read."

"I have watched my husband for seventeen years in Arkansas handle every imaginable situation. I have always been impressed and extraordinarily respectful of the ways in which he deals with problems that I think are extremely taxing."

"My husband and I have always been each other's sounding boards. Even before our marriage, when we were students at Yale."

Chelsea

"We want her to have a chance to be a normal child and to develop into the person she was meant to be. I think she'll get a great deal out of the experience, just as she has with her father being governor. But we've also never put any pressure on her. We've pretty much left the decision to participate in the political world up to her, and we're going to do the same thing when we live in the White House."

"Well, we've tried to make it possible for her to have as normal a life as possible. But it isn't easy, and certainly for my husband it's practically impossible. He can't get out and, you know, walk through the mall easily. . . . "

They both help Chelsea with her homework:
"If she doesn't have a lot of it or gets it done, we might play cards together or work on a puzzle or watch TV."

"What we try to do is to schedule this time at night to know that we're going to have dinner together and know we're going to spend time together. She and her dad like to watch terrible movies together."

Tom Brokaw (NBC News at Sunrise, January 18, 1993): "Your whole family now is going to get a lot more attention, and it's not always going to be the most pleasant kind of attention. Have

125

you talked to Chelsea about that, for example, and how has she responded to it?''

''We've told her not to talk to strangers and the press. No, really [we] have tried to give her some sense of what it's going to be like, and as her parents, we're trying as much as we know how to give her some protection from the inevitable attention she'll have as the daughter of a president.''

Katie Couric: ''Why are you so guarded when it comes to your daughter?''

''Because I want her to have as normal a life as she can, to be the person that God meant her to be. And I think that the only way that I can do that is to give her a chance to grow up as she would, nearly as possible as if her father were not the president. And that was one of the great pieces of advice that Mrs. Onassis gave me, and I've been very grateful for that advice.''

When Saturday Night Live *ran a skit about Chelsea:*

''I think it's sad that people don't have anything better to do than be mean to a child. My attitude is that I'm going to do everything I can to help Chelsea be strong enough not to let what other people say about her affect her. In her particular situation it's obviously much bigger, but it happens to children all the time. Unkind and mean things are said by people who are either insecure or going for the laugh or going for the nasty remark—whether it's on a playground or on a television set."

On the press's attention to Chelsea:

"I think that she's got a pretty clear sense that if her cat becomes a world celebrity, there is a lot of interest that is not related to anything about her, or about what she stands for or what she believes, and that she has to be able to see her way through that and make choices that are right for her."

"The best part is simply being her parents, because she's an absolutely wonderful person. Also, there's something good about having her father work near where he lives. Chelsea can run over after school or call him up, and they can see each other. And Bill's usually home for dinner, so there are some good routines that can be established that are important to us."

"I am not going to answer any questions about her. I mean, that's the way that we try to give her a normal life, is that I try to keep her privacy and respect how she lives and give her as much space as possible."

"She's a happy teenager, I think. She comes and goes pretty much as she pleases; she has wonderful friends. We've kept the press out of her life.

"That may be our only achievement so far."

Asked about Chelsea's turning sixteen:

"It's much harder for me than it is for her. She is chomping at the bit to get on with her life, you know; being sixteen, she thinks the whole world is out there, and I'm very pleased that she has so many interests and she's got great friends and [is] involved in church and school and all. But it is difficult, and thinking about her going off to college in a year and a half is much harder than I ever thought it would be. I'm somebody who cried when I took her to kindergarten."

"Well, she is still very interested in ballet. Right now she wants to learn to drive and get a driver's license, which is something I'm living in fear and trembling of, but her father, which is very scary, is teaching her how to drive. So they're having a good time."

Asked if Chelsea has her driver's license yet:

"Not yet. Not yet. This is—you know, you're talking about the party we had for her. I would hasten to add that the

128

best way to have a party for thirty-six teenagers is to have the Secret Service and the military there.''

Asked about Chelsea's learning to drive with her father teaching her:

''You know, they were doing everything from parallel parking to backing up. When I came back, I said, 'Well, how'd it go, how'd it go?' and she said, 'Well, I think Dad learned a lot.' So they really have a good time. But she'll be looking at college and I'm just not looking forward to that myself. I will miss her so much.''

Asked what qualities of her father are in Chelsea:

''Well, she certainly didn't get her math ability from me! She has inherited that from her father. And she has the same remarkable big mind and big heart.

''You know, I watch the way she's taken from both of us, and it helps me to be a better person, to improve.''

Socks

''The two most common questions that I'm asked, and they were asked today, are how is Chelsea and how is Socks. That is what I am always asked, no matter what group I'm in.''

Told she sounds fearless:

"Oh, no, no, you know, I don't like creepy-crawly things. And one of the Secret Service persons told me the other day that there were rats at the White House. But Socks'll make short order of them."

Discussing Socks during a speech at the Joint Armed Forces Wives' Luncheon, November 19, 1993:

"This has been the most traumatic part of the move for us. Because before, he could range freely and do anything. And now he has to be confined, because we're worried if we let him loose he might get catnapped. And this is a very serious concern. I don't think I can get away with assigning Secret Service agents to watch Socks, so the alternative is that we have to kind of keep him on that leash, and those are terrible pictures, I know.

"You know, those of you who love cats, to see this beautiful cat, who is really descended from cat nobility going back to the Egyptians, on this leash . . . But you will be— I mean, even with cats, things finally get better."

CONTINUING CRISES

"We were not real estate developers and Jim [McDougal] had a track record, and I wasn't a cattle expert. I trusted

Jim Blair and it worked out for me, and I wasn't a real estate expert and we lost money. Those things happen."

Talking about Madison Guaranty:

"The young attorney, the young bank officer, did all the work. It was not an area that I practiced in. It was not an area that I really know anything to speak of about."

"I sometimes don't know what I've been accused of from day to day."

"I don't believe Little Rock is some unique situation. I think if you go anywhere in this country . . . people do business with people they know. I don't understand why this had come as a revelation."

Asked about Whitewater/Madison Guaranty:

"In the current political environment where credibility is questioned and accusations are hurled over things that are perfectly appropriate, legal, but in retrospect give cause for anyone to raise questions, of course I wish that no one could raise this. It's a little bit odd that in my twenty years of law practice and involvement in so many activities, you know, I'm getting grilled over what I did, which amounted to about an hour of work over each week over fifteen months, and it was by no means important or significant to me at the time."

"I didn't think that anyone would presume anything, other than that I was trying to do the right thing all the way down the line. Right now, I'm a little confused about what the rules are."

"You know, we've been through this now for four years, and it started off as one thing, and every time a particular set of charges are disproved and questions answered, the ground shifts. And there's never any stable ground to stand on to say, 'Okay, everybody, let's take a deep breath.' "

"It's a little bit odd that here we are, both my husband and I, nearly fifty years old—which is hard to believe. We don't own a house, we own half of the house that Mother lives in, in order to help support her. He has his 1968 Mustang, I have my 1986 Oldsmobile Cutlass. A recent magazine said that with our legal bills, we are bankrupt. So, if we had intended to trade on my position, I've done a very poor job of it."

Travel Office

"There was petty cash left lying around. Cash ended up in the personal account of one of the workers. Now, that may not seem like something to people who spend lots of money, but coming from Arkansas, that sounded serious. And so, from my perspective, it was something worthy of being concerned about. Even if it was just the press's money, that money belongs to people and it should be handled appropriately if it is in any way connected with the White House."

"Although I had no decision-making role with regard to the removal of the Travel Office employees . . . I expressed my concern . . . that if there were fiscal mismanagement in the Travel Office or in any part of the White House it should be addressed promptly. I am sure I felt such action could include, if necessary and justified, appropriate personnel actions so that this administration would not be blamed for condoning any existing fiscal mismanagement problems."

"Before I came to the White House, I dealt with people in a very direct way. If something was on my mind, I said it. That is an entirely different environment, and the mere expression of concern could be, I guess, taken to mean something more than it was meant."

Commodities Trading

"Back in 1978, in October, one of our best friends, Jim Blair, who had been a friend of my husband's and mine for some time, talked to me about what he thought was a great investment opportunity. He is someone who has been an investor ever since he was a teenager, with usually very good results, and he had followed closely what had been happening in the cattle market. And I only knew a little bit about that, although living in Arkansas, particularly northwest Arkansas as I did, I was familiar with a lot of ranchers and people who were in the cattle industry. And when Jim, said, 'I think there's going to be a great opportunity to make money,' and explained why and asked me what I thought we could afford to invest, I told him $1,000. So I opened an account at his very strong recommendation and proceeded to trade over the next months until July.

"You know, not all my trades made money. Some of them lost money. I talked to Mr. Blair very frequently. In fact, Jim would call me on a regular basis, and I would make a decision whether I would or would not trade, and then the trade would be placed. Often he placed it for me. And there was nothing wrong with that. He was on the spot. He was often in the offices of the broker."

"I didn't think it was that big a risk because I thought that Jim and the people he was talking with knew what they were doing."

"I stopped trading in July of 1979, and I did stop trading in large measure because I could not keep up with it. It takes a lot of nerve to be in the commodities trading, and I just found out I was pregnant. And so when he called again I said, 'You know, I just don't want to do this anymore.' And I think he may have even called a few more times saying, 'You know, it's really still doing well. Trade again.' And I didn't, and I'm glad I didn't because he and other friends of mine who were trading ended up losing money. So it was a good investment offered by somebody who knew a lot, who could provide a lot of good advice, and I was lucky and made the decision to stop when I did."

She attributed her success to her adviser James Blair's . . .

". . . theory that because of the economy in the early part of the 1970s, a lot of cattle herds had been liquidated, so that there was going to be a big opportunity to make money in the late seventies."

"The fundamental facts have not changed. I mean, the fundamental facts are, as I have said: I opened an account with my money. I made the trades. It was nondiscretionary. I took the risk. I was the one who made the decision to stop trading. And that I did rely on Jim Blair. I used

135

some other advice as well, but he was my principal adviser in this."

Asked if she were riding on Blair's coattails:
"No, I wasn't. I was riding on the money I invested."

"I made the trades. I had absolutely no reason to believe that I got any favorable treatment."

"I can't read their minds or speculate, but I had absolutely no reason to believe that I got any favorable treatment. I don't think you'll ever find anything that my husband or I said that in any way condemns the importance of making good investments and saving. I've always believed in a zone of privacy, and I told a friend the other day that I feel after resisting for a long time, I've been rezoned."

Vince Foster

"Oh, he was one of my dearest friends, Barbara [Walters]. He was a colleague, he was a partner, he'd been a friend of my husband's since they were boys of four or five years of age, and I miss him. I miss him very much and I just wish he could be left in peace, because he was a wonderful man to everyone who knew him."

Whitewater

"The conventional wisdom about Whitewater always is take any straw you can to go on, so I don't have any doubt that there are those who will say this should go on. I just would like to tell them, go on where, we've been going on four years, and every time there's an official investigation of any sort . . . what my husband and I have been saying proves out to be the case. So I don't have any doubt that since so much of this is politically inspired it will go on almost regardless of what happens anywhere. It has a life of its own."

". . . because we signed the loan papers. So we were 100 percent liable—we and our partners; they as a couple, we as a couple, but also we as individuals. We kept putting up money every time we were asked. That's how we ended up losing more than $40,000. So it was not a sweetheart deal. We were on the papers. The bank looked to us to make good if there was any default. We had to, over the years, put in money every time our partners asked, even though we were passive investors. And at the end of the day, we lost money."

137

"We never should have made the investment. I suppose the other big mistake that I made was not appreciating how other people view their reluctance to publicly divulge information."

"[The Whitewater controversy is] a well-organized and well-financed attempt . . . to undermine my husband, and by extension, myself, by people who have a different political agenda or have another personal and financial reason for attacking us."

"We made lots of mistakes; I'd be the first to admit that."

"You know, those are things you look at in retrospect. We didn't do anything wrong. We never intended to do anything wrong."

Claire Shipman (CNN, Inside Politics Extra, January 17, 1996): "I think what's hard for a lot of people to believe looking at those poll numbers is that such a savvy, smart woman as yourself wouldn't, for example, have known the ins and outs of a land deal like Whitewater or that sort of investment."

"In 1978 or 1979—maybe it was '77—when we got into

that land deal there was nothing wrong with it. There's never been anything proven to be wrong about it. You see, the very question you ask assumes that there was something wrong about what we did. And we said, when the questions were first raised in 1992, we didn't do anything wrong. We were passive investors. We lost money."

Asked what was at stake for the Clintons:

"We shouldn't have anything at stake, if people were actually looking at the case and what it's about. There has been no implication of my husband. The only allegation that was ever made about him in the last four years was made by David Hale, who everyone, the prosecution and the defense and the people following the trial, know is an admitted crook and liar and a lot of other things, so I don't think that there is anything at stake. Obviously, we know the people involved. We are concerned about our state and the attention that this has drawn, but as to anything affecting either of us, it doesn't really matter which way it comes out with regard to us."

On an appearance on Oprah:

"I'm prepared, literally, as I've said, to climb to the top of the Sears Tower, go to the South Pole, whatever it will take to get this matter over with."

"I am just not interested in spending my days falling into the trap that the fomenters of all this want us to—which is to become isolated and on the defensive and diverted."

"People keep asking questions that we keep answering; they just don't like the answers. If they don't want to believe we lost money in Whitewater, that's their choice, but that doesn't change the truth: We lost money in Whitewater. You know, if they don't want to believe that we paid back all our loans, and we never did business with an S&L, fine, they don't have to believe it—but that doesn't change the truth. . . . They can ask me from now to doomsday—they're going to get the same answer, because it's the truth."

"We went into Whitewater to make money, not to lose it. I mean, the embarrassing thing to me is that we ended up losing money and it keeps being beaten like the deadest horse there is over and over again.

"And we didn't have anything to do with the operation or management of it. We just basically thought that eventually the payments by the owners of the lots would begin to pay us back and make a profit. And that never happened."

"I know nothing bad happened. And that's what everybody's going to know, as they should know now, since they have yet to come forward with anything but the wildest kind of paranoid conspiracies."

Asked about the Whitewater records that suddenly turned up at the White House: "How on earth did these records end up there?"

"I don't know. And I wish that they'd come out in August. I didn't know that she'd* found them. And I'm not sure she knew what she found, based on what she said yesterday. This has been, for me, kind of a difficult time because I can't answer these questions. I don't know where they've been. I wish they'd come out sooner."

"I was glad to have the opportunity to tell the grand jury what I have been telling all of you. I do not know how the billing records came to be found where they were found, but I am pleased that they were found because they confirm what I have been saying."

"I am bewildered that a losing investment which for us was significant—sixty-nine thousand dollars, which is provable by the accountants—is still a topic of inquiry."

* Carolyn Huber, an old friend and office manager from the Rose Law Firm who now works at the White House.

About the prospect of appearing before Senator Al D'Amato's Whitewater panel:

"Oh, I think it would be like having your teeth drilled. I mean, I can't imagine anything worse, you know, than—especially since you have no idea what the questions are. I mean, if I knew that they were going to ask me about X and Y that would be fine, but these people think they can come out of left field, or more likely right field, and ask me anything. So, it's not going to be a very easy experience for anyone, but I will do whatever it takes."

"I've never understood the furor over this failed land investment, and the kind of conspiracy theory people have tried to weave strikes me as kind of silly. I didn't realize that what I saw happening before my very eyes was the big-lie technique of saying something over and over again and trying to make it true. I would have been more attentive and taken the whole press inquiry more seriously. I'm trying to do that now . . . I have to be very careful to be sure the public gets the information they want so they know what happened sixteen years ago, so they know we never borrowed money from any savings and loan, and we paid everything back we ever borrowed. I'll try to be more effective explaining what happened and answering questions."

Hillary Rodham Clinton was the first-ever first lady to testify before a grand jury (investigating Whitewater):

"It's not a first I'm proud of."

142

On testifying about Whitewater:

"There is nobody who wants this over more than I do. I really want it to be finished with."

"I look forward to being able to tell the grand jury what I know, to be able to answer their questions. I, like everyone else, would like to know the answer about how those documents showed up after all these years. It would have been certainly to my advantage in trying to bring this matter to a conclusion if they had been found several years ago. So, I tried to be as helpful as I could in their investigation efforts."

Asked about her Whitewater testimony: "Would you rather have been somewhere else today?"

"Oh, about a million other places today, indeed."

Asked if Whitewater and other issues will come up in the campaign:

"Well, I hope not. It doesn't have anything to do with anything that the American people should look for in a presidential campaign. There's no factual basis to the charges, so it should not be in the campaign, but do I think it will be in the campaign? Of course, it will be in the campaign. I think everything, including the kitchen sink, will be in the campaign. So I don't have any doubt that, uh, people who are opposed to my husband will say or do anything in this campaign, which I regret, but nevertheless think will happen."

"You've got to remember that I have tried the best way that I know how to be as careful as possible. Now, in hindsight, I suppose people can say, 'You should have done this, you should have done that.' I didn't presume that anybody would presume anything other than that I was trying to do the right thing all the way down the line."

Asked what she and her husband knew or should have known:

"Shoulda, coulda, woulda. We didn't."

The Whitewater records had Vince Foster's notes on them, and people said they came out of his office:

"I can't help what people say. People have been saying things about this for four years which have been proven, time and again, to be untrue. There is nobody who wishes those documents had been found earlier than I. We've had literally thousands and thousands of boxes in Arkansas and in Washington searched for now more than two years, looking for everything that might be relevant. The law firm did not have copies of those documents. The savings and loan did not have copies of those documents. I don't know where they've been. I don't know who's had them. I don't know what has got to happen to make them appear."

Health Care

HEALTH CARE HISTORY

"You know, health care reform in our country goes back a number of decades. Some have argued that the very first proposal actually was made by Theodore Roosevelt as part of his platform when he first ran for president and then renewed it when he ran again. But we certainly know that Franklin Roosevelt talked about it being the other part of Social Security. And your own President Harry Truman was one of the most passionate advocates on behalf of health care reform.

"And then, of course, we had the changes in the 1960s, to provide Medicare for Americans over sixty-five and to provide Medicaid for people who were too poor to provide for themselves. And then President Nixon recommended comprehensive health care that was built on the employer-based system, the system by which most of us who are insured receive our insurance benefits."

"Harry Truman went to the Congress in 1945 and said, 'We have to have universal health care coverage.' That was when we were only spending 4 percent of our incomes on health care. Harry Truman saw, in 1945, exactly what was going to happen if we didn't change. He fought like crazy. He gave everything he had."

Truman introduced health care legislation in every session of Congress while he was president:

"If we had done what President Truman wanted us to do back then, we would be a lot better off, both financially and in our ability to provide every American with health care. We've been struggling with this issue for fifty years. We're going to keep on trying to get it done."

"Then along came President Nixon, who the last time I looked was a Republican. And he—I just want to tell this to all the young Republicans who are here. I want them to hear this: President Nixon introduced a bill, in 1970, to extend universal health care coverage financed by employers and employees, paying just like the Health Security Act introduced by President Clinton."

"Every president who has touched it has got burned in one way or the other because the interests involved are so powerful."

Speech to the American Medical Association, Chicago, June 13, 1993:

"But while we have talked, our problems have gotten worse, and the frustration on the part of all of you and others has increased. Time and again, groups, individuals, and particularly government, has walked up to trying to reform health care and then walked away."

"I have never seen an issue that is as complicated as this. I can see why for fifty years people have tiptoed toward this problem and turned around and run away."

THE NEED FOR REFORM

Remarks to the Congressional Black Caucus, September 16, 1993:

"Now, the president believes that insurance should carry with it a guaranteed benefit package so that every American will have access to the same comprehensive benefits. And those benefits should include primary and preventive health care. We should reverse the bias against preventive health care and insure us against getting sicker by making it possible to get care earlier and solve problems."

"We want you to be able to choose your health plan. . . . It has to be portable from job to job and across state lines. . . . We want to insure quality. . . . We do have to control costs."

"I'm not an expert on health care. I'm not somebody who has studied it or ever, you know, done any of the things that you do when you're in the system. But what I really want to do is to be somebody who helps make sure that what we come up with sounds real and will work. I mean, I want it to be understandable and workable for real Americans. I mean, I know how I feel about my doctors. I want to make sure that I'll always be able to have the doctors that I feel most comfortable with."

Speech to the American Medical Association, Chicago, June 13, 1993:

"We have looked at every other system in the world. We have tried to talk to every expert whom we can find to describe how any other country tries to provide health care. And we have concluded that what is needed is an American solution for an American problem by creating an American health care system that works for America. And two of the principals that underlie that American solution are quality and choice."

"What we believe is that when every American is guaranteed health security, as part of the ongoing education about health-related issues, we hope there will be a much greater willingness to talk about these difficult life-and-death issues before they arise in a family or individual context.

"We want very much for people to sign living wills, to sign advance directives, to have those conversations with their family members and with their doctors and other health care givers."

Mrs. Clinton appeared before the House Ways and Means Committee. She stressed the need for cooperation between Democrats and Republicans . . .

". . . to hammer out the choices that confront us [so that] every American will receive a health security card guaranteeing a comprehensive package of benefits that can never be taken away under any circumstances."

She singled out the health care effort as . . .

". . . the most important social policy that our nation will have confronted in many decades."

Speech to the American Legion Annual Conference, February 15, 1994:

"We ought to be paying for prevention. We ought to be taking care of people when they are at least able to be cured instead of when we have to do the most extreme and expensive kind of surgery or chemotherapy on them at the very end of the process."

Speech to the League of Women Voters, June 14, 1994:

"There is nothing more basic than health care, making sure every child, every person, has access to the kind of health care that you and I always seek for our own families, knowing very well as we look and hear about medical disasters that there, but for the grace of God, go any of us. So, at the end of the day, it is about our humanity, about our country, and about our future, and that's why what you are doing in fighting for health care reform is so profoundly important."

"I want to live in a country where the care of children is not determined on whether or not their parents have health insurance."

The Problems

Address at Marshall University, November 4, 1993:

"The most discriminating part of the health insurance market today is that part which services small and medium-

151

sized businesses and individuals who are self-employed. They're the ones who are paying far more than they should. Oftentimes, 40 percent of the premium for a small business goes to overhead and administration and profit. Not to health care.

"We are going to level that playing field. Small businesses are going to have the same opportunity to get cheap, good, high-quality insurance as the largest big business does."

"Let us remove the kind of micromanagement and regulation that has not improved quality and has wasted billions of dollars."

Remarks to the American Medical Association, June 13, 1993:

"The latest statistic that I have seen is that for every doctor a hospital hires, four new administrative staff are hired. And that in the average doctor's office eighty hours a month are now spent on administration. That is not time spent with a patient recovering from bypass surgery or with a child or teenager who needs a checkup and maybe a little extra TLC time of listening and counseling, and certainly not spent with a patient who has to run in quickly for some kind of an emergency."

"I know that many of you feel that as doctors you are under siege in the current system. And I think there is cause for you to believe that, because we are witnessing a disturbing assault on the doctor/patient relationship. More and more employers are buying into managed-care plans that force employees to choose from a specific pool of doctors. And too often, even when a doctor is willing to join a new plan to maintain his relationship with patients, he—or she, I should say—is frozen out."

"Although we are the richest country in the world and we have the best of medical care available in the world, we spend more money on health care and take care of fewer people than our competitors, who provide health care to all of the people and have better outcomes for the money that they spend on it. What we have instead is a patchwork nonsystem."

"Most people in this country who are uninsured get up every day and go to work. They would be a lot better off when it comes to health care if they went on welfare. What kind of signal does it send to the 37 million uninsured Americans, 82 percent who work or who are in the families of workers, to be able to say that? What kind of responsibility does that imply?"

Address at Marshall University, November 4, 1993:
"Think of the message we have sent to literally millions and millions of working Americans. We have told them

very clearly, 'If you are lucky enough to work for someone who will help you with your insurance, or if you are poor enough and down on your luck enough to qualify for government assistance, then your bills will be paid.

" 'But if you're in the middle and you get up every day and work for a living and you cannot afford it yourself, you're out of luck.' Since when should a hardworking American citizen have to go on welfare to take care of children with medical problems, because if they don't, they are out of luck?"

"Until we have everybody in the system, we will not be able to control health care costs."

Speech to the American Legion Annual Conference, February 15, 1994:

"We have the finest doctors and hospitals in the world. We can beat any country when it comes to the quality of health care we have for those of us who are able to use it on a regular basis. But we do have probably the stupidest financing system in the world for health care. We spend money on paperwork, we spend money on bureaucracy, that we shouldn't have to spend. And what the president's plan is designed to do is to simplify our system to get it to the point where we can put doctors back in charge of the system again, where they can be making the decisions, not insurance company executives or government bureaucrats, which is the way it is too often today."

*Remarks at the 1994 C. Everett Koop National Health Awards,
October 17, 1994:*

"In our system we have spent so much money and we
have spent it in so many ways that have not enhanced the
quality of health care, but have instead fed the paperwork
hospital, the bureaucracy of our financing system, and
many people could not recognize what it would mean to
more efficiently deliver the health care dollar."

The first lady condemned the health care industry's . . .

". . . price-gouging, cost-shifting and unconscionable
profiteering."

"How can we, as the richest country in the world, be the
only one of our industrialized competitors who has not
figured out how to provide health care to every one of
its citizens?"

*Remarks at the Alzheimer's Association Humanitarian Award
Presentation, April 11, 1994:*

"This is also an issue that raises as starkly as any what
we have done in our health care system that is often so
penny wise and pound foolish, that does not recognize

real costs, human and economic, of caring for people with long-term care needs. It is so unfair and really nonsensical to draw lines that say, yes, we have a difference between medical care and long-term care, and we will help your father who has a heart attack, but not your mother who has Alzheimer's."

"Too many Americans today can only get help by spending their way into poverty and then only if you put your loved one into an institution, which is usually the most expensive thing to do and the last thing that many want to do. It just doesn't make sense that that is your only option. On this issue, sound family policy is also sound fiscal policy, and to those who say—and there are many who say this—that we cannot afford long-term care in our country, I say we not only can afford it, we have to afford it. It is the most effective way to care for people and to keep families together."

Commencement address at the Duke Ellington School for Performing Arts, June 15, 1994:

"We are spending more money than we need to on our health care system. We can do better. We can actually extend health care to more people if we are more efficient and careful and if we emphasize primary and preventive health care and begin to convince people that the emergency room is not their family doctor. We can save money and do a better job."

CHILDREN AND HEALTH CARE

"There cannot be a worse indictment of a country than to say parents who work are going to be penalized when others who don't work will have their children's health needs taken care of. That needs to be fixed, and it needs to be fixed now."

"There are too many people, and there are far too many children, who do not get the care they need to have. Because when they show up at the emergency room, the first [thing] they're asked is, 'How are you going to pay for your medical care?' And if they cannot answer that with 'Insurance,' or with a Medicaid or a Medicare card, they often go to the end of the line."

WOMEN AND HEALTH CARE

"As mothers, midwives, nurses, doctors and scientists, women have blazed trails for centuries as caregivers in their communities.

"Yet despite their vital role as health providers, women historically have been treated as second-class citizens when it comes to getting good care. Diagnostic techniques, treatments and research for the most common diseases traditionally have focused on men."

"Today we have begun to recognize that women have unique health problems, unique symptoms and unique reactions to treatments. But even so, women are too often excluded from major clinical studies. For example, the leading cause of death among women in our country is coronary disease, but until recently women were routinely excluded from major coronary clinical trials."

Remarks to the World Health Organization Forum on Women and Health Security, September 5, 1995:

"Women should have the right to health care that will enable them to go safely through pregnancy and childbirth and provide them with the best chance of having a healthy infant."

"When health care systems around the world don't work for women; when our mothers, daughters, sisters, friends and co-workers are denied access to quality care because they are poor, do not have health insurance, or simply because they are women, it is not just their health that is put at risk. It is the health of their families and communities as well."

"As our nation wrestles with the health care crisis, women must help shape the agenda for change. Women must speak up so they are assured of the care and treatment they need and deserve."

"I'm convinced that with a combination of health care reform, more funding for women's health research and more responsibility on the part of individuals, we can achieve more for women's health in the next decade than we have in the last half century."

SENIOR CITIZENS AND HEALTH CARE

"We had a system to care for the elderly—it's Social Security and Medicare. What we haven't done is figure out how to provide that same kind of system for children. The more poor children we have, particularly those in the most disorganized settings, the less likely it is we'll be able to continue to provide security in the most basic sense for the elderly or anyone else."

"Probably the single biggest concern I heard across the country, from both older Americans and people in their middle years who are caring for parents and other older relatives, is that the system is biased in favor of nursing home care over other kinds, yet [Medicare] provides no help.

"We want to expand reimbursement for home health care and community-based care and begin to provide nursing home care for subacute patients who don't need to be in hospitals. Now, unless a patient is in the hospital the family shoulders the whole financial burden; therefore, many patients who could be cared for in the home remain hospitalized so Medicare will pay."

Paula Zahn (CBS This Morning, May 19, 1995): "Are you in favor of overhauling Medicare without doing it within a huge, huge, large framework?"

"I'm very scared about overhauling Medicare without health care reform, and just quickly, for two reasons. First of all, if you look at what the income of Americans over sixty-five is, the average man makes less than $15,000 a year to live on, and the average woman over sixty-five in America lives on less than $9,000 a year. I really don't want to do anything with Medicare that makes it more difficult for average Americans to get their health care needs met.

"And secondly, if you slash Medicare and Medicaid to cut the government funding, what is going to keep the hospitals in the inner cities open? What is going to prevent the costs that were carried by those government programs from being shifted onto our private insurance bills, which is what will happen? So it's not just looking at Medicare alone that we need to do. There's a right way to reduce the costs and a wrong way. And I want us to do it the right way."

"And the second big problem for older Americans in the Medicare program is there is no support for alternatives to nursing home care. We do not help people who want to keep their relatives in their own home. We want to start providing long-term care options, so that families will be able to take care of their own relatives; they will not be forced to put their family members in nursing homes if they can take care of them at home with a little bit of help. It is the right thing to do, but it is also the economically smart decision to make.

"Nursing homes are very expensive. Providing a home health aide, providing adult day care, giving some respite care to the full-time caretaker of an Alzheimer's patient, that is all much cheaper than putting the person in a nursing home. So let's start giving alternatives that will enable older people to live with dignity, and not make the nursing home the only place that we take care of older people with medical problems."

"I also have an older mother, and she is like your mother—she's independent, she lives alone, she doesn't want to be a burden. I'm grateful that she's healthy, but I don't know what the future holds. Medicare works—we should try to reform it, but we should do nothing to undermine the security it gives."

161

HEALTH CARE PROFESSIONALS

"It was very reassuring to me that there are so many good, decent, hardworking, committed people at all levels of the medical system. Yet the way the system is organized often undermines their ability to do their jobs as they would like to."

Remarks to the American Medical Association, June 13, 1993:

"Most doctors and other health care professionals choose careers in health and medicine because they want to help people. But too often because our system isn't working and we haven't taken full responsibility for fixing it, that motive is clouded by perceptions that doctors aren't the same as they used to be. They're not really doing what they used to do. They don't really care like they once did."

"Blanketing an entire profession with rules aimed at catching those who are not living up to their professional standards does not improve quality."

To the Association of American Medical Colleges:

"The government's medical education policy to date has been to fund specialties at a much more attractive rate and manner than it has for primary care. We have to make a decision as a country to reverse that."

"It is time for America to start training primary care physicians again."

The health care reform proposal stipulated a ratio of primary care doctors to specialists:

"The American people did not stand on the street corners and say, 'Give us more thoracic surgeons.' "

Solving the Health Care Crisis

"For years we have ignored the link between nutrition and health. And in all the work I've done in health care, the single cheapest way to improve health care in America is for people to eat more vegetables, fruits, complex carbohydrates, less fat, plus moderate exercise, which wouldn't cost very much at all."

When asked if she would consider taxing such unhealthy substances as caffeine, salt and sugar, she replied:

"If there is a way that you can ever come up with to tax substances like the ones you just named, we'll be glad to look at it."

At the first meeting of the task force on health care:

"I don't want you to think because I'm the president's wife it's not okay to tell me what you think. I want everything on the table."

Asked if it wouldn't have been better for the president to have hired someone who could be fired to run health care:

"Well, I suppose by traditional political standards it would have been, but I guess one of the things we keep trying to get across is that my husband feels very strongly about these issues. They are not just political issues for him to be looked at on some polling data. He thinks we need to solve the health care problem. He doesn't want to be distanced from it; he wants to wade right into it. Is it a risk? Sure, it's a risk. Am I conscious that I could get blamed or, you know, be criticized? Of course. But I think that it's a risk that my husband believes is worth taking, and I agree with him."

First appearing at the House Ways and Means Committee:

"The official reason I am here today is because I have had that responsibility [for health care reform]. But more importantly for me, I'm here as a mother, a wife, a daughter, a sister, a woman."

Speech at the Institute of Medicine Annual Meeting, October 19, 1993:

"It is a complex undertaking that we are about to begin in our country. I know no way to attempt what we are doing: to achieve universal coverage; to guarantee a comprehensive benefits package; to begin to simplify a system that has become much too cumbersome, bureaucratic, and overregulated; to attempt to begin to achieve savings and eliminate inefficiencies; but at the same time to enhance quality through better outcomes, research, and reporting of those outcomes; to guarantee choice—in fact, to enhance choice—for both the citizen/consumer and the provider/practitioner; and to inject more responsibility into the system at every level."

"We should build on the employer system. The employers contribute, those of us who work contribute, and all of us then are paying our fair share. There are no more free riders in the health care system."

FINANCING HEALTH CARE

Asked where the money would come from for the Clintons' health insurance plan:

"The savings generated through health care reform will be used to offset these costs."

"Let's take the unnecessary costs and waste and fraud and abuse out of this system. And let's spend our money where it counts—taking care of people who need it."

"We must face up to the costs in this system, and we have to have the courage to talk about that openly."

AFTERMATH

Speech at George Washington University:

"I know that the perception of the health care plan, which I fully accept, was one of big government. I understand that, and, obviously, I regret it. That was certainly neither the intention nor, from our perspective, what would be the ultimate outcome of what we anticipated."

"Certainly here in Washington one of the big mistakes was going along with the recommendation that we shouldn't brief reporters even off the record, in part because there was a legitimate concern, from both people in Congress and here in the administration, that trying to put together a health care plan to meet our original date, which was May 1, was a huge undertaking. Everybody felt that was going to be hard under even the best of circumstances, and they worried that talking about it as we went along would create all kinds of false expectations or misunderstandings. But I think in retrospect that was the wrong call."

When asked: "If you had health care to do over again . . . would you have done it differently?"

"Oh, you know, I think about that all the time, because I'm giving the proceeds from this book [*It Takes A Village*] to children's hospitals, because I just can't bear the way some children don't get the health care they need. But I think there are many things I could have done differently and many things that perhaps would have been presented better. But I also believe that it is the most controversial subject in our political life. You know, if you look at Harry Truman, it just was very hard for him and it's hard for anybody who tries to approach it. So, yes, I know I made mistakes and I know there are better ways I could have done things. And if I were to do it over again, I would try to present it better. I don't know if we'd have a different outcome, but I certainly would try."

"I'm also continuing to work on trying to find better ways to root out fraud and abuse in our health care system, so we can save money and eliminate the problems that causes, and trying to help continue the effort we started to reform the regulations that govern health care so that they can be less intrusive into the work of doctors and nurses and others. So I'm continuing to work, but not at the same level that I was before."

Asked about health care if Clinton is reelected:

"I think the president has said that he would like to try to make at least some of the changes he tried last time, like insurance coverage. He really believes that insurance should be portable, people should not be written out of insurance if they have a precondition—a preexisting condition. And so those kinds of things I think we ought to try to move on. Now, my dream is I would like to see every American have insurance, and I hope someday we'll see that, because right now we're seeing more and more without."

Causes and Concerns

THE ARTS

Asked about the cutbacks in the arts:

"Well, we will continue to do everything we can to promote the arts. I've tried to do that with a sculpture garden at the White House and the crafts collection for the White House, which is on exhibit here in New York. And we will also support the National Endowment for the Arts, because I think it's very important. The arts speak to us; they tell us who we are. And I think that, as a nation, we need that today because we're going through such a changing time."

Remarks at the opening of the Twentieth Century Sculpture Exhibit, October 11, 1994:

"Sculpture has been one of my favorite art forms ever since I was a young girl. And not simply, as lore might have it, because my first date with my husband was in the sculpture garden of the Yale Gallery, but because of

169

the way it spoke to me and what it has always meant to me.

"I know that all of you believe, as I do, that art has the capacity to provoke our imaginations. And I believe where there is imagination there is hope, and where there is creative expression there is potential for human progress. And hope and progress are concepts and ideals that are as important to us today as they always have been in the history of our country."

Speech at the 125th anniversary celebration of the Metropolitan Museum of Art, June 6, 1995:

"It is particularly ironic that those who bemoan the loss of civility and character and the loss of values in America are the first to recommend obliterating the federal agencies, in many ways cutting back on state and local support, responsibility for promoting our cultural traditions."

Books

"I remember when I read *The Autobiography of Benjamin Franklin*, I discovered things about Franklin's personal life that at the age of fourteen I was shocked by."

Don Jones, a minister at First United Methodist, had given her a copy of Catcher in the Rye *when she was fourteen. She later wrote him from Wellesley:*

"I reread *Catcher in the Rye*. I didn't like it when I first read it, but now I do."

At a 1996 gathering to celebrate publication of James Carville's book We're Right, They're Wrong:

"I'm a pushover for sweet-talking southern boys. I know where they're coming from, but I still fall for it."

Her Own Book, It Takes a Village

She hopes her book . . .

". . . will remind us that for America to be a strong, confident country, we have to start caring for our children as if we were a village in the very best sense of the word."

"Ultimately, we women must take responsibility for ourselves and our health, but many of us will need assistance and support from the village."

Claire Shipman (CNN): "How would you, as a practiced politician and policy maker, take some of those valuable lessons about how to value our children and translate them into the real world, make them a real-world possibility?"

"Well, I wouldn't start from that point. I'd start more from the point of view as a, you know, a mother and a citizen, because I think most of the changes we need to do for our children start there. I really believe that if every mother and father started talking to their children when those children were babies, and reading to those children, and giving them the attention and love they deserve, and never, ever, letting anyone physically or sexually abuse any child that they had any knowledge of—those are the kinds of things that are within the power of each one of us to do in our own lives. But, certainly, as the title says— *It Takes a Village*—I think there are responsibilities that all of us have, whether we're in the media or in politics, in government, in business, in our churches, our schools. And what I would hope would come from this book is really a national conversation about what we can do better."

EDUCATION

"I agree with those who advocate dress codes and even uniforms in some districts, because they appear to diminish the frictions caused by brand-name consumerism and gang identification."

"My husband and I both got scholarships in college and law school, and my husband has recommended more work-study and scholarship money for kids who are willing to work hard. It's the best investment we can make. Because if a young person graduates from high school and college, that's good for the entire society."

"You know, I believe very strongly in a parent's right to choose what that parent thinks is the best education for his or her child. And we have a long and proud tradition of parochial and private education in America. But we also know that the vast majority of American children will be educated in the public education system, as we have for many, many years now. So I believe that we have to support the public education system whether or not our children are in it or whether or not we have children, that even people who themselves have children who are grown up or never had children have to understand that the public education system is a critical investment for the well-being of all of us. So I would say that's why I would hope you would do it [support public schools]."

Remarks at Brooklyn College Commencement, June 1, 1995:

"I remember a novel written more than fifty years ago, called *A Tree Grows in Brooklyn*. . . . Today, we see that it is not only trees that grow in Brooklyn. We see that minds grow in Brooklyn, ideals and dreams grow in Brooklyn, and futures grow in Brooklyn. And that is why I am here, because I wanted to thank all of you for doing what you do to educate and build strong students and citizens. Clearly what you have confronted and overcome in reaching this day is considerable. Many of you in this class are older than the average graduating student around the country today.

"You are already skilled in many ways of the world, and you have already paid your dues. Many of you have worked full-time or part-time, have raised families, have taken on all kinds of additional responsibilities. And I think the motto of this college speaks to the reality of a worthwhile life—'Nothing without great effort.' Your efforts are what led you to this campus in the first place. Without great effort, without great discipline and sacrifice, you would not be sitting here today."

"Education is the best investment we can make as a country. And it has always struck me as remarkable that during the Civil War President Lincoln and that Congress started the Land Grant College program. They understood what was important for the future. We cannot turn our backs on that kind of heritage."

"We also need to be sure that every young person who wants to go to college and is willing to work hard gets the chance to do so, and is not barred for financial reasons. This is no time to be turning the clock back, to be cutting student aid and scholarships and work-study."

"You know, education is not only important for acquiring facts or knowledge. It is not only important for acquiring skills to prepare oneself for making a living. It is also about learning how to meet the challenges of one's time— how to solve problems and adapt to new circumstances. It is about building a broader understanding of our world and building one's capacity for tolerance and compassion and responsible behavior. It is about defining one's place in the world and creating one's personal identity against the backdrop of how others have lived throughout history."

Asked about education budget cuts:

"I would say that if we cannot invest in better education with our children, and instead want to cut education to give the richest people in America tax cuts, we have our values upside down and backwards.

"Development experts tell us that where women lack the tools of opportunity, children tend to be less educated and less well nourished. Families tend to be larger and poorer.

"Where women remain illiterate, we find that democratic institutions are more fragile and the environment less well managed. We know that investing in education is part and parcel of providing economic opportunity because, as capital and technology become even more mobile, differences in the quality of labor forces will become that much more apparent."

FAMILIES

"I always feel kind of presumptuous to give advice. We lead a life that in many ways is like the lives of other people who are working and raising families, but it obviously is very different. And I think the real heroes of America are those people who struggle against a lot of odds to keep their families together and to support their children in school, send that child out of that door every morning knowing that there's violence in the streets—all kinds of dangers—and try to provide a safe haven for their child even though they have to work. And I think single parents particularly are overcoming extraordinary obstacles.

"And part of what motivates Bill every day is that he wants to live in a country where we don't have so many people who have to worry about that, because he thinks it'll be better for our daughter. So it's really important to us that families be given the kind of support they need and that adults take more responsibility for their own children and recognize the relationship between their own children's lives and the lives of all these other kids around them."

"The real issue for me has always been how do we create strong families and keep families together, how do we get people to marry so they have legitimate children and how do we keep the divorce rate down, so that families that already are formed can stay together and raise children. That, I think, should be the focus of our concern, whether we're talking about welfare and how it affects the people who are the poorest among us, or actually how family formation and strengthening families really needs to be addressed at all levels of society."

In a 1995 speech at the University of New Hampshire, she cited a Republican issue, family values:

"I believe we do not answer that question just by talking about family values. We do it by valuing families, by valuing children, by valuing workers."

On Larry King Live, *May 5, 1994:*

"I was just so struck by how, in our country, we talk a lot about family values and how we, you know, want parents to take care of their children, and here I was, surrounded by people, who, by the grace of God and their own love, were taking care of children in ways that I think all of us would be proud of. And yet, all they did was talk about their frustrations and how they were forced onto welfare because they couldn't get insurance, and men who were unable to change jobs, men who can't take raises, because if they take raises, they lose the Medicaid eligibility for their children. Mothers who stood there and talked about how they'd be better off if they divorced their husbands, because then they could get government assistance. That is just wrong."

"Women and children need men to be full participants in the raising of children, and men—if only they knew—need the opportunity and joy of being those participants in their own families."

"Families are undermined when women and children lack the opportunities they need to thrive."

"It is a national shame that many Americans are more thoughtful about planning their weekend entertainment than about planning their families."

Remarks to the Child Welfare League, March 1, 1995:

"No government can love a child, and no policy can substitute for a family's care. But at the same time, government can either support or undermine families as they cope with the moral, social and economic stresses of caring for children."

"If all you do is give lip service and rhetoric to families but you don't do anything . . . to make the rearing of children a primary national priority, it's a farce."

"There should be no disagreement about the fact that the family structure is in trouble; not only here but in many parts of the world. There should be no debate that children need the nurturing and care that a stable family can provide. And there should be no debate about a commonsense

178

truth that children are the result of both the values of their parents and the values of the societies in which they live."

FORGIVENESS

"I wrestle nearly every day with the biblical admonition to forgive and love my enemies."

Speech to the National Prayer Luncheon:

"I know in the Bible it says they asked Jesus how many times you should forgive, and he said seventy times seven. Well, I want you all to know that I'm keeping a chart."

Commencement address at the Duke Ellington School for Performing Arts, June 15, 1994:

"Giving up, especially when you have the talent that you all have, is an indulgence. And you only have to look at the events of the last month to realize why it is never appropriate to give up. Think for a minute about the inauguration of Nelson Mandela.

"If there were ever a man who had reason to give up, it certainly was he. Twenty-seven years, longer than you have been alive, he spent in prison. I had the extraordinary privilege of attending his inauguration. I hope you saw much of the television coverage of that historic event. But

I want to tell you what personally made the single biggest impression on me.

"Yes, I was overwhelmed by the inaugural ceremonies, by the sight of Nelson Mandela mounting the stairs, surrounded by the military leaders of South Africa who were now part of a new constitutional government. But what really moved me and what said more to me about his greatness than anything else was what he said at a function after the inaugural, when he stood before a very large crowd of visiting dignitaries and other people from around the world and told us that he had invited to his inaugural three of his former jailers.

"Stop and think about that for a minute. I felt a rush of emotion like I have never experienced. I sat there thinking, 'This man is great because he has learned the basic lessons of what it is to be a human being filled with hope, who continues to forgive, never to forget, but always to forgive, because a hopeful heart has no room for bitterness, has no room for vengeance.'

"And I thought to myself, 'If this man in this extraordinary act of humanity could overcome bitterness and invite his three jailers to his inaugural, certainly every one of us could change our own hearts and our own minds and begin to live with that same level of hopefulness.' "

HER NEWSPAPER COLUMN

"My hope is that this column, like hers [Eleanor Roosevelt's], will prompt all of us to think more about the human dimension of our lives."

Her column will include . . .

". . . some of the funny stories; some of the rather momentous events; some of the human stories, the kinds of stories about the people who come here that nobody would ever know otherwise. I hope that it will in some small way help to bridge some of the gaps that have grown up in America today, help bring people a little bit closer."

PARENTING

"The primary obligation of both parents is to take whatever gift God gave you in the person of that little boy or girl and pay attention to that child's needs, to respond to that child, to stimulate that child, to be there for that child, and to learn the kind of personality your child has so that you're allowing your child to flourish."

"I still think we make it much too hard on parents today. Many families are working longer hours now than at any time since World War II; and even with both the mother and the father working, together they are making only as much as a father made in the fifties or sixties."

"Poor parents struggle every day to give their children the most with the least. And often they are among the best

181

parents. They know children need a secure home, strong values, consistency and love. The love can be as rich and the values as sound in the homes of Watts as in Westchester, in Harlem as in Highland Park."

"Being a parent is one of the greatest learning experiences I've ever had. I have learned to respect Chelsea as a separate being, and that has given me a greater respect for all other people."

Asked on Larry King Live, *May 20, 1996, about tools for parents to help them raise children in this difficult generation when they are facing such tremendous pressures:*

"It's really what I wrote about in *It Takes a Village.* And I will just say one piece of advice that I got as I was growing up that I've passed on in the book. You know, when I used to get into a jam, or be confused about a decision, my father used to say, 'Well, how are you going to dig yourself out of this?' And starting when I was a little girl, I carried around this mental image of a shovel. And the shovel began to sort of stand for the tools that I would want any child to have. Starting with love, attention, discipline, feelings of self-confidence that are rooted in real experience.

"Now, in my book, I give lots more examples of the kinds of tools, and as I say, you know, sometimes for me in my own life, shovels weren't enough; I needed a bulldozer [laughs]."

Solving Problems

"There is enough positive energy out there to solve problems if it's harnessed and led. We need to group and deal with problems on the front end so we don't have to pay more later—and I think the federal government could play a bigger role."

Commencement address at Drew University, Madison, N.J., May 18, 1996:

"While I'm grateful in a country as this to live among people who do disagree, to be critical of our government, to be critical of the political process, I have to confess, I get tired of hearing people blame every problem we have on government."

"As I travel around the country, there's a sense of concern by people that the Congress and the president work together to solve the country's problems—and that cuts across party lines. People stand up in meetings frequently and say to me, 'I'm a Republican, but I want health care." Or 'I'm an Independent, but I think dealing with crime is the most important issue.' So I do think there is something of a disconnection between what is of concern inside the Washington political process, including the press, and what the people are waiting for: action on these problems."

"I have advocated highly structured inner-city schools. I have advocated uniforms for kids in inner-city schools. I have advocated that we have to help structure people's environment who come from unstructured, disorganized, dysfunctional family settings. Because if you do not have any structure on the outside, it is very difficult to internalize it on the inside."

"It is easy to complain about the problems we face. It is harder but far more rewarding to roll up our sleeves and work together to solve them."

TELEVISION

"I've always loved *Sesame Street*. It was a big part of Chelsea's life when she was a little girl."

Guesting on Sesame Street:
"If you want to be healthy and strong, don't forget to eat your vegetables."

"We can have one hundred hours of television, exploiting sex, and parents go nuts if kids have their gym teacher tell them how it's done."

"We don't watch a lot of television anymore, but we might watch a special. We're always interested in nature specials or something that has to do with history. Chelsea watches *Jeopardy!* and sometimes we watch that together because you always learn something. And Chelsea and my husband watch a lot of sports—they're big basketball fans."

Issues and Answers

ABORTION

The Clintons support parental notice but oppose parental consent for abortion:

"If you can presume that a child is competent to make a decision, you still want that child to have parental guidance wherever possible. But realistically, we know that in many cases that is not possible."

"I believe in parental notification. I think there are exceptions. There are situations in which the family is so dysfunctional that parental notification is not appropriate. But in general, I do believe—I think that families should be part of helping their children through this."

"We also are doing something that I think is very important, and that is for the first time we are emphasizing family planning. We are emphasizing preventive services. I want to live long enough to see abortion rare in this country. I want it to be legal; I want it to be safe; but I want it to be rare. If we do what I hope we will do in this [health care reform] plan, which is to provide better access to family planning, we will avoid this issue in the future."

ABUSE

"I think there's a bigger problem and that is we still don't take abuse seriously enough in our country. I think that we have overburdened our social welfare system in trying to make difficult decisions about abuse, trying to reunify families when actually there's not a family to reunify. So when abuse occurs with respect to children, I believe that you should move quickly to remove the children, criminally prosecute every adult involved, both the perpetrators and those who were accessories. I believe that we have to move more quickly to make a decision whether children should be returned to a home or freed for adoption."

CHALLENGES

"Every life has challenges. Life has become very unpredictable and scary for people. And the only insurance policy you've got against whatever comes down the pike is to be as ready as you personally can be. I think that's part of what the voters have been saying to me: Nobody could have predicted that all this would happen to you. You didn't ask for it. But you were ready. And, boy, we're glad you were."

CHARACTER

"I think we ought to stand up and say that education and service do matter. They are about building character. Character is one of the anchors of society. And when we talk about character we don't just mean talk, we mean action. Building a civil society that actually lives up to its ideals. It is not that Americans lack character, it is just that society has too often stopped rewarding it. Just look around and you will see the effects of what one political scientist has called 'turbo-charged capitalism.' Consumerism and materialism go unchecked, run rampant through our culture dictating our tastes and desires, our values and dreams."

CIVILITY

"Part of what we have to do in our country is reestablish civility and decency and goodwill toward each other."

"I find it ironic that those who talk the loudest about America's loss of civility, character and values (particularly those arising from Western civilization) are often the first to recommend obliterating the agencies responsible for promoting . . . arts programs that make Sophocles, Shakespeare, Mozart and O'Keeffe available to our children."

"If people disagree with one another, let's do it in a civil, polite way. Let's not call each other names. Let's try to agree that our most important effort should be coming together to help each other. And so then I think the criticism, whether it's directed at me or anybody else, it's not going to count for very much."

CRIME

Remarks at the Ninth Annual Women in Policing Awards, August 10, 1994:

"I have to tell you, as I stand here, there is something wrong when a crime bill takes six years to work its way through the Congress and the average criminal serves only four. There is something wrong with our system."

"We need more police on the streets, we need more and tougher prison sentences for repeat offenders. The three strikes and you're out, for violent offenders, has to be part of the overall plan. We, unfortunately, need more prisons to keep violent offenders for as long as it takes to keep them off the streets."

Remarks at the Ninth Annual Women in Policing Awards, August 10, 1994:

"There is no area of security more important than one's physical security: being able to feel safe in one's own home, being able to walk down a street, send a child to the corner grocery without worrying, letting a child walk to school alone. And all of you who are on the front line every single day know what an impact crime has had not just on those who experience it directly but on the entire community."

Democracy

Commencement address at Drew University, Madison, N.J., May 18, 1996:

"In a democracy, government is the people, so renewing our faith in our government means renewing our faith in ourselves and in our ability to perfect our union."

"We won that Cold War. Now we have another challenge: to strengthen emerging democracies around the world, especially nations, such as Mongolia, that are trying hard to emulate American ideals.

"Too often we forget the struggles other people endure for the privileges we take for granted."

Speech at the Greater Detroit Chamber of Commerce, June 1, 1995:

"We all know that there are unprecedented opportunities unfolding throughout our country and around the world. We are all grateful for the end of the Cold War and the replacement of totalitarianism with democracy after democracy, in places we really didn't expect to see that flower.

"We see people all over the globe seeking to emulate our country, our democracy, our economy, and yet it is clear that despite the model and beacon we are to so much of the rest of the world, that we have many questions here at home about who we are, where we're going, and what kind of future we're building for ourselves and our children.

"We also have seen very vividly in the last weeks forces at work here and abroad undermining those values, the values that we hold dear; values of civility and community, of sacrifice and service, of peace. We see antipathy too often replacing empathy. Shouting replacing listening."

FEMINISM

"I don't think feminism, as I understand the definition, implies the rejection of maternal values, nurturing children, caring about the man in your life."

Describing her mother-in-law, Virginia Clinton Kelley:

"A feminist who would never describe herself that way. [She never allowed herself] to be demeaned or victimized or subordinated in any fashion."

FREEDOM

Remarks to the UN Fourth World Conference on Women, September 5, 1995:

"Let me be clear. Freedom means the right of people to assemble, organize, and debate openly. It means respecting the view of those who may disagree with the views of their governments. It means not taking citizens away from their loved ones and jailing them, mistreating them, or denying them their freedom or dignity because of the peaceful expression of their ideas and opinions."

Commencement address at the University of Pennsylvania, May 17, 1993:

"Freedom and respect are not values that should be in conflict with each other. They are basic American values that reinforce each other. But we cannot debate our differences nor face our mutual challenges unless and until we respect each other, men and women, young and old, across the ethnic and racial lines that divide us."

THE MEDIA

"I cannot stress too much that if I could do one thing to help children in our country, it would be to change what they see in the media, day in and day out."

"The Calvin Klein ads are merely the latest proof that some businesses are willing to push the envelope of gratuitous sex and exploitation of children as far as possible if it's good for the bottom line."

"It is such a hypocrisy for some people in this town [Washington, D.C.] to yell about our movies when we use sex to sell everything in America."

Remarks at Brooklyn College Commencement, June 1, 1995:

"We are fed, through the media, a daily diet of sex and violence and social dysfunction and unrealizable fantasies. We live too often in a disposable, throw-away society, where the yearning for profits and instant gratification overshadows the need for moderation and restraint and investing for the long term."

"I don't think there's any doubt any longer that if you give children a steady diet of what they get on most programming, it is going to distort their view of the world. But it's not just what children see on television. There's been a lot of talk about that, and people have criticized the violence and the overt sexuality and other things. It's the process of watching television. You know, if a two-year-old has control over a remote control on a TV set and spends her time switching channels and has the sense that everything is immediate, everything is instant gratification, why should that child ever put in the effort to do something that's difficult or read in order to pick up information? I really think that it's both the content and the process of television watching that over forty years now has dramatically changed how children see themselves."

Terrorism

Remarks at Lahore University of Management Sciences, March 27, 1995:

"If there is one constant we know from generation to generation, century to century and millennium to millennium, it is that change engenders fear. The bounds of terrorism, the ugly face of bigotry, and the ignorance that breeds intolerance toward those of a different ethnic or religious background are all exacerbated by the fear of change. And no nation is immune."

Talking about the Oklahoma City bombing on CBS This Morning, *May 19, 1995, she was asked by an audience member: "As
tragic as it was, we saw such great images of America and who
we are. And unfortunately, the best comes out at the worst. How
can we build on that feeling without a tragedy, all the good in
us that can come out?"*

"That's a wonderful question, you know, because today is
the one month anniversary of what happened in Oklahoma City. And I think if we will keep those images in
our minds of all those people helping, showing up to help,
the kind of outpouring of caring and bring it back home,
think about our own families, our own neighborhoods, be
willing to start treating each other with more respect and
decency, being involved in our communities through our
churches and through our schools and being willing to
stand up against people who are just negative. I'm tired
of Americans being negative. We have so much to be
grateful for in our country."

*Speech at the Greater Detroit Chamber of Commerce, June 1,
1995:*

"Now, as we saw to our collective horror, home-grown
terrorism exploding in America's heartland. I don't need
to tell leaders of this business community that too many
Americans feel their lives are out of sync. American families have always been the anchor of our economy and the
backbone of our country.

"Yet as families try to cope in today's world, they are
confronted by pressures, and burdens, and uncertainties
that really didn't even exist in many respects a few years
ago. From the fears that come with the necessary downsiz-

ing to be competitive, to the reality of stagnant wages, more and more Americans are stressed out."

TOLERANCE

Speech at the Greater Detroit Chamber of Commerce, June 1, 1995:

"One of the trends that I find very troubling is the increasing inequality that exists, not only between income groups that has been exacerbated over the last several years, but the attitudes that go along with that income inequality."

"I do believe that, as the world becomes more competitive, we also become more connected and we need to be respectful of each other, we need to learn from each other's cultures, and I think that will help us be sure that we have a global community."

At the 1995 UN Women's Conference in Beijing, China wanted to ban Taiwanese and Tibetan groups, and the Vatican wanted to bar abortion rights groups from attending:

"I don't think that it is useful to shut out certain points of view because of the country they come from or the views that are held."

VALUES

"Despite our imperfections and flaws, we have a system of government and politics that has endured because it is the best system ever devised. It was rooted in values. It understood the imperfections of human beings. It believed in education and service."

Speech at the Joint Armed Forces Wives' Luncheon, November 19, 1993:

"The challenges facing us today are not the same as those that faced our parents and our grandparents. There are common threads which run through them, that demand the best from us. And the answers, I believe, are rooted in the same values and attitudes that really have created the climate of change that America has always been able to respond to."

"American women don't need lectures from Washington about values. We don't need to hear about an idealized world that was never as righteous or carefree as some would like to think."

"When things are not going well, when life is stressful and sometimes violent, when we are stepping over the homeless, it is natural to want to go back to what seemed like simpler times. But we can't go back.

"[What we can do is] return to the old values of caring and willingness to serve and translate those values into new terms."

"But, you know, women who pack lunch for their kids, or take the early bus to work, or stay out late at the PTA, or spend every spare minute tending to their aging parents, do not need lectures from Washington about values."

Talking about the "Murphy Brown/Dan Quayle" controversy:

"I wonder if he lives in the same America we live in, if he sees the same things we see. Part of what it means to believe in family values is to value every family. . . . I wish people in high office understood the real problems people in this country face."

VIOLENCE

Asked her views on children and violence on television:

"Well, I am concerned about violence on television because I now think the evidence is absolutely proved that children who watch a lot of violence both become more violent themselves and become less sensitive to violence. We've done some experiments where two different groups of children watch television. And some saw very violent kinds of programs, unfortunately, that are too common. Then both sets of children were taken out and were shown a situation in which some children—other children—were in trouble. The children who were watching all the violence were much slower to respond. It was as though it wasn't real to them. And so I think we've done a lot of damage to ourselves—not that anybody set out to do it. I don't think there's any big conspiracy where we're going to make ourselves more violent. Just over time, it has worn down the sensitivities and released the impulse controls of too many people. So I think if we don't start demanding different kinds of television and parents exercising more responsibility—turn it off, don't subscribe to the channels that are—the most violent programs. That's not censorship; that's parental responsibility. So we can do a lot in our own homes as well."

"Well, I think one thing is to make it clear that violence against women and children is not just a domestic matter, it is a criminal offense and should be treated as a criminal offense, and that we have to do a better job of enforcing the laws in our society so that people know there are consequences to such actions."

"I am appalled by some of the video games . . .

"Some psychologists who study videos think that being an active participant in these violent video games may in some ways even be worse than being a passive observer

199

watching violent television because you are actively involved.

"I think parents should exercise as much caution over the videos that children play as we now are seeing parents doing for television shows."

"Violence is on people's minds. . . . It's on young people's minds. And it is important to give all of our people, but particularly our children, a sense of physical security. That's the first thing adults owe children in a tangible way—that they are safe and secure."

WELFARE

"I've advocated, for example, tying the welfare payment to certain behavior about being a good parent. You couldn't get your welfare check if your child wasn't immunized. You couldn't get your welfare check if you didn't participate in a parenting program, to learn how to become as good a parent as you possibly could. You couldn't get your welfare check if you didn't show up for the student-teacher conferences, and on the line. I am a big believer, as is my husband, in linking opportunity and rights with responsibility and duties."

As to the debate over welfare reform and the Wisconsin plan, Hillary Clinton was asked if she thought it made sense to force a single mother of a young child to go to work instead of staying home and taking care of the child.

"I've thought about that a lot. For a certain population trapped in generational poverty, what we've done hasn't worked. I think getting up and going to work, going to school, and having to make the same difficult decisions about who cares for your children that every other working mother has to make is a necessary step toward learning how to be self-sufficient. Yes, people who are physically able to work ought to work. Now, having said that, I think they ought to have child-care support and they ought to have some benefits to take care of their children medically. But I don't think it's fair to subsidize some people and say they shouldn't have to leave their children when millions of women do it every day."

"Our greatest energy should be spent promoting responsible parenting and independence from the welfare system—all with a view toward building strong families and creating conditions in which children can flourish."

"There is nothing new about having poor people in our midst. What is very new is that we now have the institutionalization of that culture of poverty in ways that are difficult to reconcile with the whole concept of upward mobility, change, the American dream. And so those ob-

201

servers, including Senator Moynihan, who point out that as one of our major problems, are absolutely right."

"It is important to recognize the limited ability of the legal system to prescribe and enforce social arrangements."

Rights

HUMAN RIGHTS

Remarks to the UN Fourth World Conference on Women, September 5, 1995:

"It is a violation of human rights when babies are denied food, or drowned, or suffocated, or their spines broken, simply because they are born girls.

"It is a violation of human rights when women and girls are sold into the slavery of prostitution.

"It is a violation of human rights when women are doused with gasoline, set on fire, and burned to death because their marriage dowries are deemed too small.

"It is a violation of human rights when individual women are raped in their own communities and when thousands of women are subjected to rape as a tactic or prize of war.

"It is a violation of human rights when a leading cause of death worldwide among women ages fourteen to forty-four is the violence they are subjected to in their own homes by their own relatives.

"It is a violation of human rights when young girls are

brutalized by the painful and degrading practice of genital mutilation.

"It is a violation of human rights when women are denied the right to plan their own families, and that includes being forced to have abortions or being sterilized against their will.

"If there is one message that echoes forth from this conference, let it be that human rights are women's rights. . . . And women's rights are human rights, once and for all.

"Let us not forget that among those rights are the right to speak freely. And the right to be heard.

"Women must enjoy the right to participate fully in the social and political lives of their countries if we want freedom and democracy to thrive and endure."

WOMEN'S RIGHTS
Choices

Remarks at the Pentagon Celebration of Women's History Month, March 1, 1995:

"We are, I hope, working to make it possible for men and women to make the choices that are right for them. And those choices for women should be able to include soldier or lawyer, businesswoman, teacher, homemaker, anything else that is right for them at that point in their life when they must make that decision."

"You may choose to be a corporate executive or a rocket scientist, you may run for public office, you may choose

204

to stay home and raise your children—but you can now make any or all of those choices—and they can be the work of your life."

"We ought not to be stereotyping one another, and we certainly ought not to be saying to women one choice is the right choice, and if you choose this, you're okay, but if you choose something else, you're not. That is not fair and it does a great disservice to the richness of women's lives today."

"What I have said for years and years is that I just want to live my life the way that I believe is right for me. I want every woman to have the same opportunity. I do not prejudge any other woman's choices."

"The kind of choices that women have to make today are tough choices. I'm a big believer in women making the choices that are right for them. And the work that I have done as a professional, as a public advocate, has been aimed at trying to assure women can make the choices they should make."

Keynote address at Scripps College, April 26, 1994:

"I look back now in the last twenty-five years and think about the choices my women friends have made. I have friends who are living very much like my mother did. They are full-time homemakers, full-time mothers volunteering in their communities.

"And if they feel good about their choices, then they are living the lives they were meant to live, with integrity and excellence. And I have friends who never married. Have not yet had children, although that becomes an increasing possibility as the years go by, unlike the past, and who have devoted themselves to one career or many, taking joy and enthusiasm out of everywhere they've lived, everywhere they've worked, every challenge they've met and confronted. And if they are satisfied and lived their lives with integrity, then that is the right choice for them.

"Most of us struggled to balance family and work at different points in our lives. I have friends who have had their children in their twenties. And by the time they are in their late thirties and forties are embarked on a whole new set of life experiences. I have friends who have had their careers in their twenties and their thirties and started having children in their forties. All different combinations of possibilities that are now open to women.

"And the only thing that is holding women back from realizing their full potential is their own insecurity about the choices they make in their own lives and their unwillingness to listen to the silent voice inside themselves which tells them what is the right decision for them, and not the siren calls of either praise or condemnation that come from the outside."

"In country after country, women have demonstrated that, when given the tools of opportunity—education, health care, access to credit, political participation and legal rights—they are better able to make the right choices in their lives. They can lift themselves out of poverty and, even more important, they can lift their families, communities and nations."

Address to the UN Fourth World Conference on Women, September 5, 1995:

"At this very moment, as we sit here, women around the world are giving birth, raising children, cooking meals, washing clothes, cleaning houses, planting crops, working on assembly lines, running companies and running countries.

"Women also are dying from diseases that should have been prevented or treated; they are watching their children succumb to malnutrition caused by poverty and economic deprivation; they are being denied the right to go to school by their own fathers and brothers; they are being forced into prostitution, and they are being barred from the ballot box and the bank lending office.

"Those of us who have the opportunity to be here have the responsibility to speak for those who could not."

"Now is the time to act on behalf of women everywhere.

"If we take bold steps to better the lives of women, we will be taking bold steps to better the lives of children and families, too. Families rely on mothers and wives for emotional support and care; families rely on women for labor in the home, and increasingly, families rely on women for income needed to raise healthy children and care for other relatives."

On her trip to the women's conference in China:

"To me it was important to express how I felt. I felt good about what I said."

Remarks at the Celebration of International Women's Day, March 8, 1995:

"No single factor contributes to the long-term health and prosperity of a developing nation more than investing in education for girls and women. In countries where governments have invested in primary and secondary schooling for girls and women, the investment has been repaid many times through higher economic productivity, greater participation of women in the modern labor sector, lower infant and maternal mortality rates, improved child nutrition and family health, longer life expectancy, lower birth rates, and stronger families and communities."

"All of us must participate in a conversation about how to shape the changes we seek in the world we share. It is particularly important that women find their own voice and become participants and decision makers in the home, the workplace, community, and nation. We must develop a new language to replace the deafening silence that still sounds too often when women's concerns are raised."

Remarks to the UN Fourth World Conference on Women, September 5, 1995:

"We need to understand that there is no one formula for how women should lead their lives.

"That is why we must respect the choices that each woman makes for herself and her family. Every woman deserves the chance to realize her God-given potential.

"We also must recognize that women will never gain full dignity until their human rights are respected and protected."

"No one should be forced to remain silent for fear of religious or political persecution, arrest, abuse or torture.

"Tragically, women are most often the ones whose human rights are violated."

"The fortunes of our women are inextricably tied to the fortunes of our global community. If women don't thrive, the world won't thrive."

"As long as discrimination and inequities remain so commonplace around the world—as long as girls and women are valued less, fed less, fed last, overworked, underpaid, not schooled and subjected to violence in and out of their homes—the potential of the human family to create a peaceful, prosperous world will not be realized."

Women's Roles

"As women today, you do face tough choices. You know the rules are basically as follows:

"If you don't get married, you're abnormal.

"If you get married but don't have children, you're a selfish yuppie.

"If you get married and have children but then go outside the home to work, you're a bad mother.

"If you get married and have children but stay home, you've wasted your education.

"And if you don't get married but have children and work outside the home as a fictional newscaster, you get in trouble with the [former] vice president."

"Over the past two and a half years, I have been privileged to meet with thousands of women all over the world. And I am convinced that no matter where we live, all women share a desire for strong families, economic security, legal rights, better health care and education, an end to violence and an opportunity to realize our own potential. Too often, the most pressing concerns of women are dismissed as marginal. In fact, these 'traditional' women's issues hold the key to progress and prosperity. Our global future depends on the willingness of every nation to invest in its people, especially women and children."

"We're all in it together. That's the way I feel. Every woman I know is struggling with these same challenges and issues."

To a group of gifted high school students:
"There's that kind of double bind that women find themselves in. On the one hand, yes, be smart, stand up for yourself. . . . On the other hand, don't offend anybody, don't step on toes, or you'll become somebody that nobody likes because you're too assertive."

"If we take bold steps to better the lives of women, we will be taking bold steps to better the lives of children and families, too."

"I believe with all my heart that women are the world's greatest untapped resource, and that that resource is too often being wasted today, but that each of us in our own lives and in the lives of those we can touch can begin to unleash the full power and glory of that resource."

"I have often thought of myself and my friends as transitional figures. Maybe more sure of where we were coming from than where we were going. And friends of mine have described our coming-of-age as being on the cusp of changes that fundamentally redefined the role of women."

Frank Sesno (CNN, Late Edition, March 19, 1995): "You have pointed out that women bear the brunt of poverty and illiteracy around the world. Talk a little bit about that and what is being done and what you would like to do to change that."

"Well, you know that's true in our country as well, that the poorest of the people in our country are single women with their children, and that is a pattern that, unfortunately, holds throughout the world."

Remarks to the UN Fourth World Conference on Women, September 5, 1995:

"As an American, I want to speak up for women in my own country—women who are raising children on the minimum wage, women who can't afford health care or child care, women whose lives are threatened by violence, including violence in their own homes.

"I want to speak up for mothers who are fighting for good schools, safe neighborhoods, clean air and clean airwaves.

"For older women, some of them widows, who have raised their families and now find that their skills and life experiences are not valued in the workplace . . . for women who are working all night as nurses, hotel clerks and fast-food chefs so that they can be at home during the day with their kids . . . and for women everywhere who simply don't have time to do everything they are called upon to do each day.

"Speaking to you today, I speak for them, just as each of us speaks for women around the world who are denied the chance to go to school, or see a doctor, or own property, or have a say about the direction of their lives, simply because they are women."

"I recognize that discussion of such problems as education and health care for girls and women is viewed by some as soft, labeled dismissively as a woman's issue, belonging, at best, on the edge of serious debate about all the problems we confront on the cusp of the twenty-first century. I want to argue strongly, however, that the questions surrounding social development, especially of women, as discussed at the recent social summit in Copenhagen, are at the center of our political and economic challenges."

"A woman's role in the family is that of the primary care-taker, and I think that is a role most women feel comfortable with and which their husbands are most supportive of and feel comfortable with as well."

Remarks to the UN Fourth World Conference on Women, September 5, 1995:

"It is also a coming together, much the way women come together every day in every country.

"We come together in fields and in factories. In village markets and supermarkets. In living rooms and board rooms.

"Whether it is while playing with our children in the park, or washing clothes in a river, or taking a break at the office water cooler, we come together and talk about our aspirations and concerns. And time and again, our talk turns to our children and our families.

"However different we may be, there is far more that unites us than divides us. We share a common future. And we are here to find common ground so that we may help bring new dignity and respect to women and girls all over the world—and in so doing, bring new strength and stability to families as well."

Women and Work

Remarks at the Ninth Annual Women in Policing Awards, August 10, 1994:

"If, as for most of us in today's world, the choices we make include both family responsibilities and work responsibilities, then we ought to be able to expect the respect in both the home and the workplace that that balancing act requires.

"There should no longer be any room for anyone undermining or criticizing a woman's choice, if that woman is choosing what is best for her. And all women ought to support each other so that all of us are able to fulfill our own potential and achieve the level of personal security that comes from knowing we are doing what we want to do as well as we are capable of doing it."

Remarks at Lahore University of Management Sciences,
March 27, 1995:

"In my own country, I have seen single mothers who are raising children alone while holding down several jobs. I have seen women professionals bumping up against the glass ceiling, unable to fulfill their own potential in their professions. I have seen women around the world planting crops, plowing fields, taking goods to market, running health clinics and schools, caring for orphans and neglected children along with their own, managing businesses, dispensing justice and doing the hard work for bleeding nations. Investing in the health and education of women and girls is essential to improving global prosperity."

"Then there's the vast majority of us who are trying to balance family and work. The first thing I think one has to do is to give up any idea of perfectionism, which is hard, particularly for women who have been achievers. You have to be tolerant of yourself and what you're capable of doing in twenty-four hours. Then you have to set priorities."

"I think that it is an extra burden that we carry to be able to fit into a workplace that is based on values and experiences that we didn't have much role in shaping, but in which we want to make our contribution."

"You know, the work that I've done as a professional, as a public advocate, has been aimed in part to assure that women can make the choices that they should make—whether it's full-time career, full-time motherhood, some combination, depending upon what stage of life they are at. And I think that is still difficult for people to understand right now, that it is a generational change."

Remarks to the UN Fourth World Conference on Women, September 5, 1995:

"The truth is that most women around the world work both inside and outside the home, usually by necessity."

"It is important for women to earn their own income, even when they are married."

Asked if she has advice for young women wishing to combine a career and family:

"Yes. Do what you think is right for you. And that may mean making some compromises at certain points in your career in order to care for your children, but it's worth it. We're going to live so much longer now as women. We've gained thirty years of life in this century alone, and there's plenty of time to have a family and work that you care about."

At a tea for German women leaders in politics and the arts:

"The balance between work and family, which is difficult, should be understood and supported. And it is only when we do that, that we will break down the stereotypes that affect women's lives so that individual women will have the right to make whatever choice is best for them."

"If women could have four months to be full-time mothers and then some flexibility on the job, we could move back and forth more easily between our roles."

"The same standards are not applied to men and women . . . you know, the woman who is tough and aggressive and adopts a male management style gets penalized because she's not acting like a 'lady.' The woman who adopts a more collegial management style is not thought to be tough enough to move to the highest levels of management."

"We need to create concrete help for families so women have the option of staying home at certain stages of their lives and have better-paying jobs when they work. Too many working mothers are among the working poor."

Children

"Nothing is more important to our shared future than the well-being of children."

"Let's not fool ourselves. National policies, whether they are about education, health care, work, welfare or anything else, are mirrored every day in the lives and experiences of our children."

"Unlike stocks and bonds and commodities that are traded in a market which is out there to be invested in—and you can see the immediate return; you either make money or you lose money—our children deserve a much more careful and long-term investment."

Maria Shriver (Today, *January 16, 1996): "What's the most important lesson that you've learned since you've been first lady from children and about children?"*

"That we aren't paying enough attention to them, and they desperately need our love, our attention, our discipline. You know, I get letters, Maria, that just would break your heart—they break mine—from children who have been abused, whose—one or the other parent has abandoned them, who have terrible illnesses . . . and they're not getting treated. And there's a general sense that I get from talking, particularly to teenagers, who are usually a little more able to discuss these things than younger children, that a lot of our kids just feel like they're not the top priority in adults' lives and even in the adults around them."

Remarks at Lahore University of Management Sciences, March 27, 1995:

"Every nation must reward their own people and especially their children. The boys and girls that represent the future of humanity—and to the extent possible, nations—that can help people in other nations should do so, because enhancing the human potential anywhere in today's interconnected world enhances it everywhere."

Remarks to the Child Welfare League, March 1, 1995:

"Children were protected by labor laws beginning in the 1930s. Congress appropriated funds for emergency maternal and infant care in 1943. The National School Lunch Act was passed in 1946 after it became evident that many inductees into our armed forces in World War II suffered from poor nutrition as children.

"Throughout much of our history, children's programs have received broad bipartisan support because there is such compelling evidence that early intervention saves money and lives, and reaffirms the values of opportunity and responsibility that built America."

Remarks at the Elie Weisel Humanitarian Awards, April 14, 1994:

"As unthinkable as it may seem, over the last thirty years conditions have actually worsened for American children ages zero to three. Yes, we have made progress, and we can point to it and take pride in it, but as Elie Weisel has reminded us often, our technological and scientific progress has outpaced our progress as moral beings, and that is certainly true when it comes to the treatment of our children."

"All of us have to recognize that we owe our children more than we have been giving to them."

She once complained that the . . .

" . . . debate in the U.S. about the importance of a better

221

life for our kids too often results in shouting, not shedding light, and generates heat and hate.''

''Let us acknowledge that when it comes to the treatment of children, some individuals are evil, neglectful or incompetent, but others are trying to do the best they can against daunting odds and deserve the help only we—through our government—can provide. Let us use government, as we have in the past, to further the common good.''

''For some young children, abuse may be the only attention the child got; so when you remove it, there is an extraordinary guilt: 'I must have done something really terrible because now they do not even want me.' ''

''On the eve of the twenty-first century, American children are growing up in a world where competition for jobs is more intense than ever, where health care in our country is too costly, where college tuitions get higher and higher, and where poverty and neglect are increasing instead of decreasing.''

''It is just extraordinary, unbelievably unacceptable, that any child anywhere in our country would be playing in a park and have to cope with a stray bullet and then be left with medical needs that cannot be met in a society that permits that to go on."

Speech to the American Medical Association, Chicago, June 13, 1993:

"All of us respond to children. We want to nurture them so they can dream the dreams that free and healthy children should have. This is our primary responsibility as adults."

She denounced . . .

". . . the unbelievable and absurd idea of putting children into orphanages because their mothers couldn't find jobs."

On Newt Gingrich's suggestion of putting poor children in orphanages:

"I doubt either mom would have given up Bill or Newt without one heck of a fight."

"If we do our part in our professional lives and in our personal lives . . . this country will again be able to say it is fulfilling the most fundamental obligation that any generation has, to care for and nurture the next."

Speech before the Children's Defense Fund:

"We owe our children more than we've been giving them. What on earth could be more important than making sure that every child has the chance to be born healthy, to receive immunizations and health care as that child grows?"

"I feel sorry for some kids I see. I think children who get too much freedom too soon are bewildered by the amount of freedom when they are too young to exercise responsibility. There are too many kids in the sixth, seventh and eighth grades left alone at malls and allowed to stay out late. I don't think it's good for children. . . . A child has to have an opportunity to make mistakes so she can mature. Trying to find that balance is the history of good parenting, and all of us are struggling to meet it."

"There are many ways of helping children. You can do it through your own personal lives by being dedicated, loving parents. You can do it in medicine or music, social work or education, business or government service. You can do it by making policy or making cookies.

"Not for one more year can our country think of children as some asterisk on our national agenda.

224

"How we treat our children should be front and center of that agenda, or I believe it won't matter what else is on it. My plea is that you not only nurture the values that will determine the choices you make in your personal lives but also insist on policies that include those values to nurture our nation's children."

CHILD CARE

In 1990, in the position of board chair for the Children's Defense Fund, Hillary Rodham Clinton joined a study team of child-care professionals for a two-week visit to France:

"What we saw was a coordinated, comprehensive system, supported across the political spectrum, that links day care, early education and health care—and is accessible to virtually every child.

"[France thought of its children as] a precious national resource for which society has collective responsibility. Mandated paid parental leave for childbirth and adoption acknowledges society's obligation to nurture strong parent-child ties."

"Child care is not just a family matter. To do our children and our country justice, we need to develop a nationwide consensus on how to best nurture our children, and, through that nurturing, prevent the personal and social costs we all pay when children's needs are not met.

"Before we lock ourselves into a makeshift, inadequate

child-care policy, we ought to consider valuing children, French-style."

CHILDREN'S RIGHTS

Quoting her article, "Children's Rights: A Legal Perspective, in Children's Rights: Contemporary Perspectives, *edited by Patricia A. Vardin and Ilene N. Brody (Teacher's College Press, 1979):*

"The first thing to be done is to reverse the presumption of incompetency and instead assume all individuals are competent until proven otherwise. . . . Yet the law basically treats all . . . children, at their dissimilar stages of life, as incompetent."

"I have seen a lot of situations in which families have abdicated their responsibilities to their children. At some point a child's rights deserve careful attention, and some parents do not deserve continued authority over their children. I know there's a lot of debate about this, and I was criticized during the '92 campaign for my 1973 article about children's rights, but anyone who has dealt with abuse knows that at some point you've got to make a very tough decision."

"Family disagreements that result in legal battles are, of course, of a more serious nature. The most recent example of disagreement between parent and child is found in the abortion cases recently decided by the United States Supreme Court. The Court held that a minor child might seek an abortion without her parents' consent and over her parents' objections if a court believed it to be in the child's best interest.

"Decisions about motherhood and abortion, schooling, cosmetic surgery, treatment of venereal disease or employment, and others where the decision or lack of one will significantly affect the child's future should not be made unilaterally by parents. Children should have a right to be permitted to decide their own future if they are competent."

From a 1973 essay titled "Children Under the Law," written for the Harvard Educational Review:

"The phrase 'children's rights' is a slogan in search of definition. Invoked to support such disparate causes as world peace, constitutional guarantees for delinquents, affection for infants, and lowering the voting age, it does not yet reflect any coherent doctrine regarding the status of children as political beings.

"Asserting that children are entitled to rights and enumerating their needs does not clarify the difficult issues surrounding children's legal status. These issues of family autonomy and privacy, state responsibility, and children's independence are complex, but they determine how children are treated by the nation's legislatures, courts, and administrative agencies.

"The capacities and the needs of a child of six months differ substantially from those of a child of six or sixteen years."

Said about a scholarly article she wrote in 1973, while still a student at Yale Law School, examining the murky area of children's rights:

"There is no way that anybody could fairly read the article and say I was advocating that children sue parents over taking the garbage out."

Our Changing World

Speech at the Greater Detroit Chamber of Commerce, June 1, 1995:

"There is a sense that nothing is really permanent in our society anymore, not families, not neighborhoods, not jobs, not even our values. And so instead of the working class or the middle class, we have now in our country what is being referred to as the anxious class. And I'm talking about hardworking, responsible men and women who because of shifting employment trends have been forced to change jobs, maybe to take on an additional job. Many people who drive too far to work and get home too late. People who worry about whether they can afford to take care of their aging parents while sending their children to college. People who are struggling to keep their businesses and their dreams alive."

"The world itself has undergone dramatic changes. Around the globe, communism has given way to capitalism, tyranny to democracy, closed markets to open ones, all of which is forcing us to redefine how we define ourselves and the human experience."

To the Association of American Medical Colleges:

"Change makes people anxious. My husband is very fond of saying that people always are in favor of change in general, but not often in particular; and I think that in today's current climate that is certainly true. People know things have to change, but they are just not sure what directions or what specifics the change should take."

Remarks at Lahore University of Management Sciences, March 27, 1995:

"We are all struggling to adapt to new challenges without giving up a sense of who we are, where we belong. People are fond of saying that the world is growing small, and in many ways it is smaller, when we all have real hard access to information and ideas and each other, to the media and computers. But that experience of immediacy can also be unsettling, creating within and around us a stressful state of rapid transition and dissolution, over which we have little control."

Looking to the Future

Commencement address at Drew University, Madison, N.J., May 18, 1996:

"On the eve of this new century and millennium, our task as Americans is to work together to perfect our union, just as those before us have done. Our task is to respect our political process and our democratic institutions and respect each other when we feel strongly opposed to points of view, nevertheless to treat each other with civility. Because we know we are granted privileges and rights here in this country that others have died for and continue to die for."

"Now every generation faces challenges. We are on the brink of not only a new century but a new millennium. A thousand years ago there were many who thought the world was coming to an end. We had hit rock bottom in the human experiment with little hope for our future. But look at what happened in the last thousand years, not only medicine, science, industry and technology advanced, but we saw human civilization attempting step by step to overcome our own flaws."

Address to students at the University of Colorado, March 14, 1994:

"So this is really a struggle for the future. It's a struggle for determining who we are as a people. We have, I believe, the will to meet that challenge. But the only way we can do it is for each of you to take a hard look at yourselves where you are in your lives and to know that the kind of country we will have for you in the future depends upon the decisions we make today."

Speech at Keene State College:

"None of us can predict what the next year or the next century holds for us individually or for America, but one thing we know with certainty is that if we meet the challenges that confront us, we are more likely to make the future better for ourselves and our children."